About the Author

M. D. Herter Norton, an accomplished violinist and violist, appears to have been destined from a very early age to become an authority on the art and technique of playing string quartets. Her first teacher of violin was Ludwig Marum of the Marum Quartet. At the age of eleven, she spent a year in Frankfurt am Main studying with Fritz Bassermann, violist of the Herrmann Quartet, the leading German quartet of its day. In New York, at the Institute of Musical Art (now the Juilliard School of Music), she studied with Julius Roentgen, second violin of the Kneisel Quartet, and worked in the summertime in a quartet with Louis Svečenski, violist of the same quartet, and with other artists. She also had quartet instruction from Franz Kneisel, leader of the Quartet, and spent many hours attending its rehearsals.

For two years Mrs. Norton taught string quartet playing at the Manhattan School of Music. She has always carried on an active interest in quartets and quartet playing and has published, with Roy Harris, an arrangement of Bach's Art of the Fugue for quartet. More recently she has been serving as violist in the chamber music classes of the Wilton (Conn.) Music School, which is under the direction of Lieff and Marie Roemaet Rosanoff. Mrs. Norton's home is in Wilton.

OTHER NORTON PAPERBACKS IN MUSIC

Gerboth, Walter, et al., Editors, *An Introduction to Music: Selected Readings*
Mann, Alfred, *The Study of Fugue*
Parrish, Carl, Editor, *A Treasury of Early Music*

SOURCE READINGS IN MUSIC HISTORY
Selected and Annotated by Oliver Strunk

Antiquity and the Middle Ages
The Renaissance
The Baroque Era
The Classic Era
The Romantic Era

THE ART OF
String Quartet
Playing

Practice, Technique and Interpretation

With 132 Examples in Full Score

by M. D. HERTER NORTON

With a Preface by ISAAC STERN

The Norton Library   NEW YORK

W · W · NORTON & COMPANY · INC ·

W. W. Norton & Company, Inc. is the publisher of current
or forthcoming books on music by Gerald Abraham, William Austin,
Anthony Baines, Sol Berkowitz, Friedrich Blume, Howard Boat-
wright, Nadia Boulanger, Nathan Broder, Manfred Bukofzer, John
Castellini, John Clough, Doda Conrad, Aaron Copland, Hans David,
Paul Des Marais, Otto Erich Deutsch, Frederick Dorian, Alfred
Einstein, Gabriel Fontrier, Karl Geiringer, Harold Gleason, Richard
Franko Goldman, Peter Gradenwitz, Donald Jay Grout, F. L.
Harrison, A. J. B. Hutchings, Charles Ives, Leo Kraft, Paul Henry·
Lang, Jens Peter Larsen, Maurice Lieberman, Joseph Machlis, W. T.
Marrocco, Arthur Mendel, William J. Mitchell, Douglas Moore,
Carl Parrish, John F. Ohl, Vincent Persichetti, Marc Pincherle,
Walter Piston, Gustave Reese, Curt Sachs, Adolfo Salazar, Arnold
Schoenberg, Denis Stevens, Oliver Strunk, Francis Toye, Donald R.
Wakeling, Bruno Walter, and J. A. Westrup.

Dedicated
to the memory
of
THE KNEISEL QUARTET
1885–1917

Preface by Isaac Stern

As I TOUR WIDELY over the country, I have been observing with the deepest satisfaction the growing love, understanding, and *practice* of chamber music. This growth has been particularly marked in college and university communities. Not infrequently one finds a resident professional string quartet coaching and inspiring the many undergraduate, graduate and faculty groups that meet together regularly to make music. But even where no professional quartet is found, amateur quartets seem to abound, and their standards of performance are often surprisingly high.

This interest has been reflected heretofore in the vastly increased publication and sales of recordings as well as of a number of good books on the history and analysis of chamber music. It is really surprising, however, to find that Mrs. Norton's book is the only one available for competent direction to the *player* (as opposed to the listener) of string quartets.

And it is most fortunate that the only book on the subject should be so good and so serious a one as this. It is in a very real sense a pioneering work, for there is not available in any language, to my knowledge, a well systematized work on the technique and interpretation of that marvelous body of music called "the string quartet." Mrs. Norton realizes, as do all musicians who have practiced the art, that there are difficult and fascinating technical and interpretative problems in it quite different from (even when related to) the musical problems of other kinds of performances—even chamber music combinations other than the string quartet.

What she has done in this excellent little book is to codify the problems and offer various guides to their possible solution. These guides, rather than hard and fast answers, are ones that have been handed down by tradition, a tradition that she traces very briefly in the book. They have stood the test of time, as has the great musical literature from which she quotes again and again to illustrate her points. To own, study and refer repeatedly to the

7

guide should save many hours of work for any serious group of players in achieving the highest musical goals of which they are capable, for it will avoid, in many difficult passages, the hit-or-miss methods which are, alas, so often more miss than hit. By illuminating these difficulties this book could lead them, from a sound basis, to feel freer to start the exciting path of musical discovery, the glorious search for beauty that is the great joy of chamber music.

Perhaps what the book does *not* pretend to do is just as much a tribute to its integrity as what it does so well. Mrs. Norton does not attempt to show the reader how to be a fine and sensitive musician. No book could do that by itself. What it does is to show the player with an adequate technique how he may express the best that God and his own good taste have endowed him with. The use he makes of the fine and subtle points scored in these pages is then up to him and to his three companions in music.

Contents

ONE

Style and the String Quartet

THE STRING QUARTET may well be called a phenomenon. It is, after all, a self-sufficient instrumental form so satisfactory that it has survived by virtue of its own qualities for a couple of centuries and has a good chance of continuing to do so as long as instruments are played upon by people. Many of the greatest composers have cast their finest ideas in its mold, and many distinguished players have found in it a vehicle for their highest achievement. No apology is needed, then, for any attempt to define its style and explore the technique of its performance.

Exactly how this particular form came into being out of the welter of trio-sonatas with *basso continuo,* quartets for various combinations of instruments and quartet-symphonies for various numbers—just why, too, the clavicembalo was dropped in favor of the string family alone—may remain forever unexplained. It took Haydn a while to make his way into real string quartet composition: indeed, it is not known whether some of his early "quartets" were intended for just four players or were really quartet-symphonies for a small string orchestra and usually performed with clavicembalo. The first "String Quartet" by Mozart (K. 80)—whom we later find, at sixteen, waiting out rainy hours in a coach station on his third Italian journey, composing a "quartet" out of boredom—was certainly not yet a string quartet in our sense.

11

Even while these efforts were going on—as late as 1777, indeed—Monsieur F. de Castillon, *fils,* declared in the supplement to the great *Encyclopédie des Sciences* that while there might be a real *quartet* of four solo parts each with its own tune, "it would be so confused that the most practiced ear would have much difficulty to distinguish each voice. The best way to make a real *quartet* is to put it in the form of a fugue or canon." What would Monsieur de Castillon, *fils,* have thought of the *Grosse Fuge,* the great fugue of the big Bb Quartet, Op. 130, for which, even in 1826, Beethoven agreed to provide a lighter substitute to please his publisher; or of those other free forms of his which gave an impetus to developments that are to this day unexhausted? String technique grew apace in those years, meeting the composers' increasing range and in turn offering them further possibilities to draw on. The string quartet—which Beethoven referred to all his life as a "violin quartet" —has been, and still is, an excellent medium for experimentation, and in its literature the many styles of music are represented.

Being so compact and lasting a form, the string quartet has developed a style of its own—and this in two senses. First, there is the style of the music. One might attempt to define style as an element that governs the composition of music and itself pervades all elements in the music, what Alfred Einstein calls its "inner bearing". This implies the final crystallization, all technical elements perfected, of the composer's musical thought. And since the medium of the string quartet does not afford such variety and brilliance of instrumental color as the orchestra does, composition for it becomes the more dependent on the inherent musical ideas, as though the notes themselves took on more individual significance; indeed, one might say that the very limitations imposed upon the medium by its range and refined homogeneous texture serve to intensify the significance of the musical style.

Second, there is the style of the performers, which is the very quality into which their powers have crystallized and which enables them to carry out and give expression to the musical style. It is the outer bearing, as it were, that reflects the inner.

With these two aspects of style—the composer's and the performer's—string quartet playing is concerned in its own way. It involves on the one hand a literature of the most clear and perfect specimens of musical thought and on the other the blending of four individual and equally important personalities into a performing unit.

Interpretation of a work, then, depends upon an understanding of string quartet style. Many years ago Louis Svečenski, that wise and gentle viola member of the Kneisel Quartet, would meet enthusiastic reports of some visiting organization, based on its performance of a (then new) Hindemith or Bartók, with a little smile: "And how was their Haydn?" This remains a good point to remember, for while we have since been developing a background of familiarity with the music of Bartók, let us say, which should enable us to judge the stylistic values of a performance *as* Bartók, we cannot forget how exacting in its own way the good performance of a Haydn continues to be.

There is obviously a *right* style for any given composition: Beethoven demands other qualities than Haydn; Debussy and Ravel, with their multiform *pianissimi,* than Brahms the red-blooded. We find that one quartet group excels in playing Beethoven, another in French works, another in certain moderns. There is naturally a temperamental inclination of the individuals making up a quartet, as with individual artists, toward one type of music or another. While this may be based in part on schooling (to the extent that different schools of string playing still exist), it is also likely to rest upon national and racial elements which become characteristic of a person's playing. Everyone knows the lilt in the Viennese waltz, the lift and rush of a Hungarian dance, and how a person of one temperament may perform them better than one of another. Everyone can understand, too, how it is that a Latin may not feel ready sympathy for Brahms, and so forth. If certain national characteristics may limit a given player's conception of other styles, they are in turn indispensable to a true presentation of music in his own national style. Not that a quartet of Russians, let us say, who have never been beyond the borders of the USSR, could not give a fine performance of a Beethoven quartet or the Debussy, or that a Western group could not deal successfully with Borodin or Shostakovitch. But it would be only natural for the nationality and training of the players to influence their interpretation and style of performance.

Tradition helps retain the distinguishing features of a style. The terms "tradition" and "right style" do not imply a conservatism that admits of no change. We know that works which seemed difficult early in our century, because they differed from classical and romantic patterns and used unfamiliar harmonies and unaccustomed effects, are no longer so forbidding to the older generation and have became second nature to the young. Of course we ourselves are also contributing to what will eventually be tradition. Traditions, as each generation passes them along, are guidelines to the understanding of the styles to which they relate, and to ignore or break these or get them tangled does something hurtful to the music. There are "traditions" which have changed, we like to think, for the better. Today we are scandalized to learn, for example, that in the first performance of Schubert's D Minor (Death and the Maiden) Quartet—from manuscript and in the composer's presence—cuts were made. Even twenty years later, when Schubert was long dead and his works were being performed in public for the first time by the Josef Hellmesberger group, the most distinguished in Europe, not only were cuts still made, but light pieces by other composers were often tossed off between movements. And when the famous Müller Brothers' Quartet gave a series of serious quartet evenings, they dared only occasionally and with much hesitation to place a single movement of a late Beethoven quartet between other numbers on their program. Surely we need not hesitate to feel that our tradition today of respecting the composer's intentions— not to mention the "tradition", less than a quarter century old, of *not* applauding between movements—is more fitting.

On the other hand, it is true that audiences today would not sit through the endless programs—any more than as families they would consume the endless meals—that used to be served up in earlier times. Today composers tend to write shorter symphonies and quartets than they did in the 19th century, partly inspired, perhaps, by the exigencies of broadcasting, perforce a highly time-conscious activity which may also account for such score markings as "22 min." and "4 min., 20 seconds". But since our general proclivity in all manifestations of this mid-century life is toward speeding things up, even the interpretation of music is, unfortunately, often affected by this sense of haste through a tendency to *play too fast*, a tendency deplored by our best and wisest musicians. For what happens when we hear a quartet pitch into a late Beethoven as though it were a race to the finish line? With hasty tempos, where is the mellowness, the meatiness? Or when the finale of the Haydn D Major (Fig. 85)—*vivace*, after all, means "lively, animated, brisk, somewhat exceeding *allegro*", but not especially fast—is taken *prestissimo* and rattled off like a virtuosic *perpetuum mobile* for the first violin? The little counter-theme in the minor, with its off-beat accents, hardly has room to take shape; its character, its graciousness are gone, its style is wiped out. What is gained when in these ways tradition—and style—succumb to the "spirit of the times"?

There are two useful sources of tradition. One might be called *theoretical*: concerned with general knowledge of the composer's ideas, his nature, his times, the artistic features and state of instrumental technic of his period, giving the student fundamental reasons for his own conception. The other is *aural*: hearing the interpretative descendants of those who played with the composer's direction or approval. Vienna, the home of Haydn, Mozart, Beethoven, Schubert, Brahms, and so many others, in that golden age of music produced a long line of violinists, conductors, critics, whose influence has been and will be felt far down the years. Both Schuppanzigh and Mayseder played Beethoven's quartets under his direction. Schuppanzigh gave the first performance of the Eb, Op. 127, but when it proved a failure, Beethoven handed the task over to Böhm and worked with his quartet in their rehearsals. Böhm, in turn, was the teacher of Hellmesberger, whose son Josef led the famous quartet of that name, while Joachim also had his early quartet-playing experience with Böhm. The traditions established by the great European quartet players of the 19th century have come down to us through their students and through younger men who heard them play. Today, while it is much to be regretted that America's first great quartet—formed by the first-desk artists of the Boston Symphony Orchestra, all of whom stemmed from these European traditions, under the leadership of Franz Kneisel—preceded the era of satisfactory recording, we can still listen to records of thirty or forty years ago by the Flonzaley, the Léner, and a few other quartets.

A certain discrimination is needed in dealing with this second sort of tradition. Every player has his own personal style, also his personal idiosyncrasies. Schuppanzigh—who taught Beethoven violin and viola, played quartets with Prince Lichnowsky, and became the leader of Count Rasoumowsky's quartet—was grotesquely fat, and it is said that in his later years he could not reach the higher positions on his instrument! Mayseder's manner of playing seems to have been small and fine, like his own style of composition, and it is recorded that Beethoven was never altogether satisfied with his work. An interpretative artist may not necessarily play at all times or all his life, in a given manner. Furthermore, changes and developments in technique, in musical conceptions and performance as they have led to our own day must be understood, so that music may be allowed to meet the test of time without sacrificing its distinctive character.

The creative mind objects, perhaps, that it needs respect no tradition, being a law unto itself. But it cannot disregard the achievements of creative genius that have preceded it. The very style in which a music has been created provides an inherent tradition, inescapable, but also invaluable to the player, who not only creates but re-creates. Tradition is a guide for him, not a law. He is at liberty to alter it when he can prove good and sufficient reason for the triumph of a new way. Mendelssohn told the youthful Joachim, who felt hampered by the then still valid custom of not using *spiccato* in classical compositions: "Go ahead, my boy, if it suits the passage and sounds well." Artistic individuality *is* free to do as it chooses, provided it has learned that accuracy which, as Emerson said, "is essential to beauty". Meanwhile a healthy respect for tradition may save it from the dangerous idea that mere tampering with recognized custom projects a new or significant light on the music.

Now, before it can attempt to interpret musical style, a quartet must master the essential style of its own form. It faces a set of problems distinct from either solo or orchestral problems. Quartet playing means four individuals who must make a unified whole yet remain individuals. The soloist is a whole in himself, and in the orchestra individuality is lost in numbers that are held together by the personality of the conductor. The stringed instrument technic through which the quartet functions must serve effects that are special to this medium. For phrasings, bowings, fingerings, *pizzicati*, all means of color production take on a new significance in quartet music. Experimentation in this field, often by trial and error, is one of the joys reserved to the true devotee of this art.

The purity of quartet style demands the absolute subjection of virtuosity to the music, and while the best technical equipment is not too good for it, the skill of the player will be tested rather by his treatment of a passage in relation to the rest of the parts than by any outstanding brilliance of execution. It is well known that the great violinist is not necessarily a successful quartet player; his individualistic vitality, noble though it be, may disrupt the spirit of ensemble music. Even four equally accomplished virtuosi do not constitute a quartet: the *mere* virtuoso remains hopelessly foreign to quartet style, while one who naturally grasps the musical intention may have difficulty in fitting his exuberance into the whole. Good quartet playing gives the best possible training in all-round musicianship, since it requires adaptability to others, as well as clear and understanding performance on the part of each member.

It is amply evident that after all their study and experiment no two quartet organizations turn out alike. We have every sort, from the "knock-'em-dead ensemble" with its "accidental noises" to the most refined, the "aristocratic".

Each has acquired its own personality. Each has its own way of working. The student and the amateur have a wide variety of playing styles to learn from.

Even the experienced quartet player is amazed, when he comes to set them down, at the infinity of musical details to be particularly considered from the point of view of quartet style. But very little has been written on this subject, and that little, for the most part hidden in journals and dictionaries, is not easily available to the interested.[*] The present volume is an attempt, not to perpetuate any given theories that would fix dynamic matter in a rigid mold, but rather to awaken curiosity, the inquiring, not easily satisfied habit of mind, the creative sense which does not take what lies before it for granted, but contributes its own sensitive approach to its objective by constructive triumph over mechanical problems. The choice of examples has intentionally been limited to certain quartets that have withstood the test of time as fine specimens of quartet writing; and the same works have been repeatedly drawn on in order to reduce the number of scores to be consulted to a conveniently small and standard one.

[*] Most writings on quartet playing are of a general historic or descriptive nature, not technical. Cobbett's two-volume *Cyclopedic Survey of Chamber Music* (London, Oxford University Press, 1930) lists in its bibliography a good letter to the Editor of *Music and Letters* (Oct. 1922, iii, 329) on "How to Practice a String Quartet" by Egon Kornstein of the then Hungarian Quartet, but fails to include J. Wharton Sharp's articles on "Quartet Playing" in *The Strad*, 1907-1909 (vols. 18-20, nos. 216-220, 223-229). It also lists *A Progressive Method of String Quartet Playing* in two parts (New York, G. Schirmer, Inc., 1924) in the form of quartet pieces with an illuminating introduction by Alfred Pochon of the Flonzaley Quartet. In 1935 Jenö Léner published *The Technique of String Quartet Playing* (London, J. & W. Chester, Ltd.), also with music, exercises and commentary. In August 1938 *The Etude* (vol. 56, no. 8, pp. 499-500) published an interview with Adolf Busch on "The Art of Ensemble Playing". An excellent little book, *The Playing of Chamber Music*, by George Stratton and Frank Allen (London, Oxford University Press) appeared in 1935, the third chapter of which is "A Performer's Analysis of Three String Quartets", namely, the Mozart C Major (K. 465), Beethoven's Op. 59, No. 3, and the Debussy.

It is the purpose of the following analysis, then, to suggest ways of getting at the characteristic problems of quartet playing and of working them out. It was undertaken in the hope that such a study might be of use to the student musician in the service of his art and to the amateur in penetrating further into the realm of things he holds so dear.

TWO

Ensemble

THE GENERAL PRINCIPLES of playing together, as epitomized in the string quartet, would seem fairly obvious: style, homogeneity, and the happy blending of the individual players' distinctive qualities. It is naturally more satisfying to listen to a professional group than to four chance artists who play without quartet style, because an interpretation is alive and interesting only when subserved by a highly developed understanding and subtlety of ensemble. This is not to disparage an impromptu private get-together of fine instrumentalists, or such performances as the Beethoven Association* provided, when one had the opportunity to hear several great artists—after a once-over understanding

* This post-World War I association was originally organized, with the purpose of performing seldom heard works of Beethoven (and behind this lay the idea of uniting a divided world through its artists), by a group of musicians and music-loving citizens under the presidency of Harold Bauer. Six concerts were given during the season, other music than Beethoven's also coming to be included on the programs. The artists contributed their services, the proceeds being used for worthy causes: benefit of needy musicians, financing of the publication (1923) of H. E. Krehbiel's translated edition of Thayer's three-volume life of Beethoven. These concerts were of a rare and refreshing distinction, and the dissolution of the Association in 1940 a loss to the musical community of New York. Something of the atmosphere they created may perhaps be experienced in our own day at summer schools of music where, away from the pressures of professional concertizing, artists have an opportunity to enjoy each other's company in playing together before an intimate audience. If quartet performances of this sort lack the amalgamation of habitual companionship, they have other values to offer.

21

rather than rehearsals—playing together for the society's own good causes, nor the achievements of a serious and skilled group of amateurs. Only that quartet style is not easily achieved, and the homogeneity that sounds so simple depends on many details which cannot be worked over or appraised without much critical thought; while the roles of the individual personality in the performance and of the instrumental voice in the composition involve subtle and various problems subject to much understanding study.

The abstract quality of music, almost too evanescent for an actual setting down in words, too dependent upon individual genius to be reasoned about or taught, makes it difficult to particularize the constituents of a good ensemble without becoming pedantic. Yet only by analysis can we begin to clarify the study of playing together. The divisions into which the subject has here been separated are made only for the sake of such an analysis and should be studied always with the realization in mind that any division is more or less arbitrary and that this divided matter is constantly interactive and interlinked.

The first requisite for a good ensemble is that each player shall have *the sense of the whole*. This he can only feel by *listening to the others*—constantly, whether he knows the music or is reading at sight. With practice, then, he becomes familiar with the other parts and is ready to adjust himself to them or to assert himself so that they can adjust themselves to him, but he can never afford to stop listening. Only by remaining acutely aware of what is being done about him can he be sensitized to the necessary degree. In reading, this is the only way to make the most of unfamiliar matter, not only following his own part but being quick to perceive its bearing upon the other parts. The poorest reader is the one who tries for all the notes regardless of the general gist of the music, while the best is alert to the new structure, harmony, voice leading, and takes an intelligent if not always a note-perfect share in the whole. In performance it is the only way to achieve the necessary give-and-take, to play in and out, to respond freely to the others' interpretations, to meet the unexpected. For circumstances condition the best-prepared perform-ance: weather, acoustic properties of strange places (which may make it very difficult to hear each other and know whether one is taking up one's own part of the ensemble properly), and the influence upon the individual's playing of his own nervous and temperamental state.

Think of the forward motion of music as of a river. Tempo, as we shall see, is the current. Each player should feel his voice a tributary stream winding in and out and in again, part of a greater whole. He must *enter without beginning* and *cease without stopping*. He should feel as though that whole were emanating *from his own mind*, only his fingers being limited to his particular instrument.

This sense of the whole should be helpful to the amateur who is not at ease in reading and who is afraid to lose his place. If, while he is busy with his own part, the rest of his mind remains alert, he will achieve a background aware-ness of what his colleagues are doing, and this will not only be of value in the ensemble, picking up cues, enchain-ments, etc., but will help him find his place if he gets "out". He should not at once throw up his hands and stop the music because he is out. Why does one get out? Usually because one stumbles at a passage or a rhythm, miscounting through some momentary inattention or some special excite-ment, some confusion or lack of understanding of the music. By listening to the others the lost one may fit in again. The leader, or some other player more secure than himself, will give a "one", or count the beats of a measure, or call out a measure number coming up or a dynamic mark to guide him; or he will hear a theme, a figure, a *piano* or a *forte,* something that gives shape to the music. Instead of giving up immediately, he should keep his eyes on his music, listen to the others and try to fit in.

There are various relationships within the ensemble that help the player in his listening. The first violin and the cello provide the frame or outline, as, respectively, chief melody-bearer and bass. The two violins, twin instruments carrying the upper voices—though the first moves for the most part in a higher register, and the second is occupied with inner-voice figures or accompaniment—frequently work together. The second violin and viola, again, form a central team as they move, together or antiphonically, in their middle-voice functions; while the cello, bass to all the rest, and the viola, as one of the lower voices, have many similar functions and often work as a pair. Each instrument, then, establishes a relationship with each of the others as well as with the whole. In reading, these relationships also may be a helpful guide.

The playing of a quartet requires just as much *vitality of interest* as any solo performance. The student may consider the second violin or viola part merely subsidiary, and his indifference will promptly show itself in monotony. He should not forget that every voice needs *convincing quality,* that accompaniment or the color of an inner line of harmony is just as important as the most melodious theme. He is the medium of an expression more extensive than his one part. If he listens well and feels the whole, he will know in his own mind the meaning of his part; then he will listen to himself more critically to be sure the meaning is clear to the listener. His own playing will ripen with this experience, and the quartet will sound better, clearer, easier, more free.

The more technical aspects of ensemble will be discussed in detail in the following chapters, but meanwhile it is essential that each player should have a *proper appreciation of the role of* his instrument, the more fully to understand and enjoy his function in the quartet.

The First Violin

By tradition the first violin is the leader. In early compositions this was necessary because he had practically a solo part, with the cello for bass and the inner voices for accompaniment and filling out the harmony. Although the inner voices have grown always more independent, adding solo to their harmonic and color importance, until in late Beethoven and in most modern music there may be little distinction in interest between the parts, still the first violin, carrying the highest voice, naturally the most brilliant, inevitably retains leadership.

This does not mean a relentless predominance. A first fiddle without the grace to subside when the music indicates that it should is objectionable and far from the spirit of quartet playing. Just as it expects to be yielded to, it should itself be ready to yield the floor when another takes the leading voice or the vital tones in a modulation. Its role may become one of commentary to the theme in another voice (as so often in Beethoven: for example, in the *Adagio molto e mesto* of Op. 59, No. 1, where the cello takes over at the ninth measure, and again, twenty-one measures before the end, where the second violin has the leading voice). Again, when it moves in octaves with another instrument which now carries the characteristic color of a passage, its more penetrating tones should not obscure the lower voice. It must be ready to drop down into insignificance, feeling itself a part of the general color and texture, just as constantly as the others do.

Its leadership among the more equally distributed parts of modern quartet music is perhaps due to the fact that, though quartet playing is a highly cooperative art, there must still be a focal point around which performance can center. The cello's function as bass, its deeper and slower-vibrating tones, make it less suited to provide this point; an inner voice can less appropriately give indications, save where these concern its own role; and because of the music itself, if any of these three acts as leader, he runs the risk of making his part disproportionately prominent. Thus, while the most experienced musician in a group will naturally be its guide, whichever his voice, in performance the greatest responsibility for holding the ensemble together devolves upon the first violin, the most brilliant voice of the four.

When devotees—whether professional or amateur—get together for an evening of quartets, it is natural for the violins, if they are at all evenly equipped, to take turns "playing first". If a group meets frequently, or regularly, with intent to work seriously at its music, a process of natural selection takes place, and thus it works out that the more accomplished fiddler takes first, so that the players are assured of getting all they can out of the combination. In a professional organization, however, the presentation of a perfected ensemble is better served if the violinists remain each in his own part, as was demonstrated by the experience of the Flonzaley Quartet. When they began rehearsing and playing in private for Mr. de Coppet, Adolfo Betti and Alfred Pochon frequently alternated, but when they went forth into public performance, Betti became the permanent first violin.

Some people are born with a "first violin personality". Others may have to learn to become good leaders. The responsible first violinist needs to be familiar both technically with his part and mentally with the whole of the music, *to practice his parts* and *study his scores*. For the amateur joining his friends in a casual evening of recreation, this may not always be feasible. But for a group that meets regularly, practice and study are most desirable, if not, as in a professional group, essential. A rehearsal with the leader unprepared is likely to be time wasted. For unless the guiding spirit of the quartet (and, we repeat, this may not necessarily be the first violin) knows what is to be done, he cannot focus the playing to any useful purpose. With his own part well in hand, he can advise with his colleagues about theirs; with the music in his head, he can mold the playing to his satisfaction.

It is not to be taken from the foregoing that the first violin is necessarily an autocrat, the big boss who goes it alone. Not at all! Each member of the group will from his own angle, contribute to everybody's understanding of the whole. Joseph Joachim, that first violin in the grand tradition, used to refer to his quartet as "our little four-voiced republic", and this is the spirit in which leadership finds its true expression. The artist who has knowledge commands the respect of his colleagues. In what concerns the personal equation, while a conductor may handle his organization like a dictator, the leader of a string quartet needs tact, above all things, to unite effectively and sympathetically the three other personalities engaged with him in the pursuit of those high aims of which quartet music is symbolical.

The Second Violin

The second violin is often considered the least interesting of the four parts. It may perhaps be called the humblest, but that does not mean that the ambitious fiddler can afford to turn up his nose at it. In so select a combination as the string quartet, each instrument is *ipso facto* as important as the others. Being the same instrument as the first and therefore less distinctive in color than the others, the second violin is a little everybody's servant. Yet its part has, ever since the earliest quartets in which all the other three accompanied the first, always consisted of more than accompaniment and bridging; in late Beethoven it has its share of musical and technical difficulties, and in modern music it partakes of virtuosity with perhaps the added difficulty that it is still a middle voice.

It must be adaptable toward the first violin, the cello or viola when its role is accompaniment or underlying voice, but on the other hand, while it should not sound out aggressively, it should speak with conviction where it has the solo voice. Having a part, one might say, of less initiative and more adaptation, of less evident responsibility, it should beware the danger of falling ever so slightly behind the tempo, as it may easily do when subdued for a considerable space. Its responsibility is there: a weak or slow second, a rough or insensitive second, can be a great misfortune. Its art is to keep alive and sensitive, to show authority when called upon to do so, to be prompt and definite, ready to bring out a thematic bit or to emphasize a harmony, a few linking notes, a supporting passage, and then to slip back smoothly into the fabric of the whole. In fact, too, the second violin part provides a vantage point from which to listen to the whole while participating in it.

The Viola

The viola is valued for its unique color. In the ensemble literature of the great composers it has grown in importance—Brahms, as is well known, had a particular fondness for it; he played it, and so also did Mozart, Beethoven, Schubert, Mendelssohn. Nowadays it is not only a composer's instrument in chamber music (Hindemith, Quincy Porter and others play it) but it has been developed as an effective solo instrument as well. It is the bond between the upper and the lower voices of the quartet, its flexible tone mingling well with the violins and also with the cello, but distinct from them: a bond and simultaneously an individual with a quality of its own. It adds flavor to the inner harmonies and a new character in solo sound: rich, sombre, emotional, sometimes hazy, sometimes nasal, with what someone has called a "remote and melancholy timbre of the lower strings when muted". A sense of these qualities, then, in addition to the requirements of adaptability, is essential to the good violist. He is the lower-middle pivot of the whole, to which he, too, listens from his own special angle.

It is fortunate that three of the four members of a quartet should be able to play each other's parts, for thus they may acquire more understanding of the whole ensemble. One can usually detect the violinist in the viola player *pro tem,* however, because he handles the viola as though it were a violin. This may go for a passing evening, but to work into the real role—the tenor, third voice, intermediary, or however one wishes to call this deeper-toned instrument—requires a special approach to tone production, to such problems as fingering and bow pressures in the grading of its characteristic sonorities. The study and practice of solo viola music is of help in this regard, in making one feel at home on the instrument and engaging one's mind with its qualities or its problems. The violinist, in turn, will find that some experience on the viola will benefit him even on his own instrument.

Learning the viola's alto clef should not present difficulties although, since we generally lack the facility our forebears had in deciphering their various clefs, the confirmed violin player may at first find it confusing. The surest and the most satisfactory way to learn it is not by any fancifully contrived system, but directly, *for itself* and *on the instrument* (as one, after all, originally learned the violin clef). If the violin-minded player goes adrift he can always find points of reference* by which to rescue himself.

* Since the instrument is tuned a fifth lower than the violin the relative position of the finger lies a fifth higher; middle C takes 3rd finger on the third string instead of on the fourth. Or there is the simple observation that the note on the middle line of the staff is middle C (it looks like violin B but sounds in the next-lower octave).

But all such rationalizings are personal, each individual will find his own, and they sound more complicated than helpful when described in words. The important thing is to *place* oneself on the viola so that one *thinks* in its own terms and not in transpositions from the violin.

In most of the "classical" literature the viola part lies low enough to remain in the alto clef, but with Brahms, for example, there are sudden departures into the violin clef, with corresponding returns into the alto. At such points the inexperienced violin-player violist is apt to lose his bearings; habit asserts itself, makes him feel he is actually playing on the violin. He has not the advantage of the cellist, who must move in and out of the tenor clef but is still handling the same instrument. It is well to practice reading high alto-clef notes until one is comfortably familiar with them (and need not take fright at a 3rd-position G, 4th finger on the A string). At the same time one should accustom oneself to their treble clef equivalents, feeling out where they lie on the viola. Then when the eye registers these more familiar treble notes, the response of hand and finger will remain more steadily at home in the *feel* of the viola. Persistence and experience, together with one's interest in bringing out the characteristic qualities of the instrument, will soon overcome any hesitation.

The Cello

The cello provides the groundwork and underpinning of the quartet structure. In the main it furnishes the bass line and the chord form. But it does much more. It came into the family—via the violone, contrabass of the viols—to reinforce the accompaniment supplied from a figured bass by the cembalo, organ or harpsichord in large or small instrumental groups, and did not begin to appear as a solo instrument until late in the 17th century. Haydn, at least by the time of the Op. 20 quartets, discovered its tone "as something more than a mere amenable bass to the harmony"; with Mozart, especially in the three "Cello" quartets (in D, K. 575, Bb, K. 589, and F, K. 590, dedicated to Frederick William II of Prussia), came fuller development of its possibilities, the differing tone colors of its upper and lower registers; and Beethoven bestowed upon it its full share, which it has since kept, as a solo and ensemble member of the string quartet.

The cellist has to bear in mind that low tones are *slow-vibrating* and that he needs to achieve a flexibility in his tone production which is malleable in the ensemble. Because of the various functions he is called upon to fulfill, furthermore, such pliancy will help him to cultivate the possibility, to which he must always be sensitive, of varying his tone quality according to the requirements of his part in the composition being played, whether as bass—and what type of bass—as solo, or as part of the inner workings of the music.

He must proportion his greater voice to give and take with the others and not let his larger instrument become too loud or ponderous. The slower vibrating of his lower tones, particularly, often makes it necessary for him to be ready to start an entrance almost a fraction of an instant sooner than he might be inclined to do, in order to sound simultaneously with the higher voices. In certain cases, too, it may be necessary for the bass tone of a chord to be set going a fraction of an instant before the others.

Since together their parts constitute the outer framework of the music, the cello must always be in such rapport with the first violin as practically to anticipate its indications. Also, as bass pivot of the quartet, the cellist is so situated that he hears the other instruments blended as they cannot hear themselves, and his point of view is accordingly of great value in perfecting the ensemble.

Into these four characters, then, four personalities are to be fitted. The expression of fresh, live individuality is a *sine qua non* of making music. But in a quartet the artistic contribution of each member will be measured by his skill in asserting or subduing that individuality which he must possess to be at all interesting. An indifferent voice, as of a weak personality, makes the ensemble totter; a too vigorous voice has the same effect, albeit from opposite causes. Personality should be distinct but not aggressive, gracious but not timid. The virtuoso is apt to have habits too individualistic to make a good chamber musician; the orchestra player, on the other hand, drilled in an aggregation, may have lost a certain spontaneous self-assertion. It does not matter in which voice the failing appears; if it appears in any the whole suffers. The happy union of personalities lies in correlating the well-proportioned virtues (and the well-controlled vices) of each of the four.

While to attain the skill required of a professionally performing organization it is necessary, as we have seen, for the violins to keep each to his own part, in the quartet-playing experience of students an interchange of instruments is desirable. The second violinist should have the opportunity to project himself into the different manifestations of the leading voice and feel the quartet from that angle. The first may make a good leader but if he cannot play a satisfactory second, he is not a good ensemble player. Similarly, while the violist type is a distinct one, to develop the viola role, it is important that violinists and violists should acquire a knowledge of each other's parts. Feeling the whole from the pivot of another characteristic voice greatly widens one's general conception of the music and develops the subtler qualities that lead to a sympathetic ensemble. It also quickens the understanding and the critical faculties. No fiddler, after all, can hear himself as others hear him, and the quartet player is dependent upon the suggestions of each and all of his colleagues in building up what he himself cannot judge in the ensemble.

It is not for us here to go into the history or discuss the merits of different schools of violin playing. All good fiddling today stems from mixed roots—Italian, French, Belgian, German, Austrian, Hungarian, Russian—producing a generally high standard of technical accomplishment through which the temperament and powers of interpretation, national and personal, of the artist and of the teacher will always, we trust, be enabled to function. It is obvious, however, that to cultivate the *homogeneity* so necessary to a good quartet ensemble the four players should have a certain type of schooling in common. A similar technical and musical background leads to a similarity of approach to the problems involved. Besides the necessary left hand agility, fundamental characteristics desirable in any executant are, of course, a relaxed performance, an easy and variable vibrato, freely controlled tone production, clean and smooth shifting from one position to another, a well-disciplined bow. There is, on the other hand, a tense style of playing which gives rise to a tight, nervous vibrato that produces a pinched tone, not full but with a sharp quality liable to affect the intonation, as well as a cramped and awkward sort of shifting that tends to let intermediate tones be heard, or too much sliding, which, as will be seen, is not desirable in quartet technic. The two types of schooling do not mingle well since they lead to different results in tone production, phrasing, etc., and one would hardly expect players so differently prepared to be sympathetic in their points of view on the execution, in the whole or in details.

The quartet player by profession knows the difficulties of finding the right group of personalities, quite apart from artistic and technical equipment. The amateur knows the discomfort one inharmonious player can inject into a gathering. Whatever the prerogatives of the leader, a quartet is, as we have said, a cooperative enterprise, and unless four persons can sit at a rehearsal with a common ideal and in an understanding spirit, they can produce neither a perfect nor a sympathetic ensemble.

Seating and Position

Quartet organizations are not unanimous about the way to place the instruments. Precedent is not necessarily significant if one recalls that Louis Spohr stood while his colleagues sat; the virtuoso could perhaps not bring himself into a more modest unity of purpose. Joachim had the cello at his left, second violin opposite and viola right of second. The Kneisels followed this pattern, which seems to have been usual in their time. The Flonzaleys placed the second violin on the first's left, viola opposite first and cello on viola's right, and this has come to be the more usual arrangement today. But the Vegh Quartet, for example, puts the cello opposite the first violin, the second violin on the first's left, and viola on cello's right, an arrangement that appears rather graceless until one gets used to it, but against which nothing can be said since the results are satisfactory.

There are arguments in favor of all these. One violinist finds that his link with the bass seems closer if the cellist is seated beside him, another that the balance is best with the cello across the way; second and viola may produce more effective ensemble when side by side, or, again, the catty-corner position may tie the quartet together better. The important points to consider are 1) that the first violin and cello should be able to communicate closely with each other, given the slower vibrations of the bass tones the latter must set in motion; and 2) that the second violin and viola, which provide much harmonic color and middle-voice unity in accompaniment and in the fractional handing back and forth of motives, should be able to function in close teamwork.

Proper seating is important. The players must be able to hear and to watch each other easily. The four stands—metal ones interpose less bulk between the players than most wooden ones—should be grouped as closely as possible, set low enough so that the players can see over them but not so low as to make them hold their instruments at a drooping angle. The two players at the rear should sit not too directly behind their front colleagues, but so that their instruments face, partially at least, toward the audience. In short, the formation is more nearly a semicircle than a square, the first violin presenting his right side to the audience, his opposite colleague his left.

Chairs

Chairs should be near enough to the stands to avoid straining the sight, far enough to leave comfortable playing space for the instruments. Since anatomies vary it is hardly practical to prescribe any given type of chair, though in public performance, at least uniformity helps appearances. At home, the simplest usually proves the best, only let it be solid; the inevitable body motion of a seated player, no matter how well controlled, is hard on antiques. The violinists' body weight should, as in the standing position, incline perhaps a little to the left, leaving the bow arm free; the left leg the more forward of the two, the right dropped a little so as not to interfere with the bow; back straight, supported at the base by chair back, if so desired, but never all the way up and never slouching, as this interferes with the freedom of the arms and gives an indolent aspect.

The cellist should face in the main toward, not sideways to, the audience, so that his tone may carry directly forward.

Lighting

Lighting sometimes presents a problem. Individual lights fastened to the stands, above, below, or at the sides, are usually unsatisfactory; they are clumsy and they generate heat. A single standing lamp with a wide shade may work well, provided it does not shine in anybody's eyes, either players' or audience's, a situation easily enough remedied (at home) by pinning a bit of paper or cloth to the shade. Ideal, if available, is a single standing lamp with four separate brackets, so that each player has his own light, but one with two brackets (stood fore-and-aft, not abeam, so as not to interfere with bows) is also practical.

Good Form

Good form is important not only for the morale of the players but for the sake of appearances, since an audience is subconsciously affected by an agreeable arrangement and an orderly performance. The player who has a rest while others are carrying on should never sit back, slouch or appear to have for the time slipped out of the picture; doing so may distract the listeners' spirit of concentration as well as that of the other players. The first violin gives his signals by a slight upward or downward motion of his instrument, or, better still, by a tiny gesture of his head, sometimes just the raising of his brows, and unity of action is helped by a look or a slight familiar move, significant to those concerned, scarcely or not at all perceptible to the audience.

Above all, eschew mannerisms. At home or on the platform. Sit quiet, feet on floor. Don't sway or weave (warning to violins if seated beside each other: from a little distance this activity makes the fiddles' necks seem about to interlock). A soloist can afford, within the limits of good style, to give his normal manner free play, but four seated players only produce a restless and disturbing effect if they indulge in a variety of independent gesturings. It is not necessary to come down with both feet for a Beethoven or even for a Bartók *sf*. Expression, emphasis, should be conveyed within the compass of fingerboard and bow and not by an overanimated torso. Not that the players should look or feel stiff or repressed; simply that they may remain calm in their preoccupation with the music, which should claim all their attention.

Counting

It is bad form for any member of an ensemble to beat time with a foot. This attracts attention and can be particularly disturbing because people's reaction-time varies so that no two are likely to beat the same rhythm in exact simultaneity. More important, it indicates uncertainty of rhythm in the player's mind; for, though rhythm may be held to originate in visceral regions, it must, to be effectively conveyed by bow or fingers, pass through the controlling certainty of that mind. Such foot motion causes an unconscious waste of nervous energy detrimental to relaxation; the brain should communicate its impulses to finger and bow, not to extraneous outlets. Of course somebody will stamp on the floor to hold things together in rehearsal or in a difficult reading. And of course, until you are very sure of yourself (and even then, perhaps, in dangerous passages), you will secretly twitch a couple of toes inside one shoe. But in principle counting should be done *inside one's head.*

One can gradually form this good habit, which is a matter of concentration, so that eventually counting loses its terrors. At first, as in reading an unfamiliar work or in practicing a passage, it is helpful to subdivide the beat, as we were taught to do in our early years; in a slow 3/4, for example, to count "1-and, 2-and, 3-and". This, being as a rule more logical in conveying the rhythmic pulse than counting "1-2-3-4-5-6-", will prevent the shock of hearing a colleague loudly say "5" when you have yourself arrived quite correctly at "3". Musically speaking, one should free oneself from these preliminaries as soon as possible, otherwise one is liable to be so busy clinging to subdivisions that one loses the flow of the phrase.

As for conventional time signatures in eighths, one has only, by an opposite process, to figure out the basic groups in the measure that carry the rhythmic pulse. That of 6/8 is usually felt in 2 groups of 3, that of 9/8 in 3 groups of 3, that of 12/8 in 4, and so on. The more tricky-looking 5/8 frequently falls into 2 groups, 1-2-3-, 1-2, and 7/8 into 1-2-3-4-, 1-2-3-; or these groups may be reversed, or some other arithmetical variation found to fit. It is the musical nature of the phrase that dictates the groupings in the measure (which explains also why 3/2 is usually read as 3 x 2 quarters, but 6/4 as 2 x 3). And if this is not susceptible to any of these groupings, a situation more apt to occur in modern than in classical music, then one has simply to count the eighths, distributing the accents as called for.

It is often well to count in eighths, or in whatever is the smallest time-value prevalent in a piece, for the purpose of steadying the tempo all round, or for fitting short note-values together correctly (cf. Ex. 4, p. 56). For example, where a dotted eighth followed by a sixteenth occurs against other sixteenths ; and the same with triplet figures. In passages of sixteenths or triplets a slight accent on the first note of the group, especially on the accented beats, has a steadying influence on the course of the whole—a very slight accent, be it noted, which in many instances comes through sufficiently if it is only in the mind of the player. Points of this sort will of course be discussed in rehearsal and procedure agreed upon so that all four players are working with the same intention.

THREE

Rehearsing

How OFTEN THE MEMBERS of a quartet meet, how much they rehearse, will depend on their own attitude and interest. Some will simply want to get together and read, as best they can, not caring too much how well they deliver the goods. Others will want to dig deeper, to give and get out of each meeting as much as possible.

Similarly the question of individual practice ahead of time, of preparation of parts, especially for the first violin if he is to be a helpful leader, will be answered by each group in its own way. *Desirable* it is, of course, for then one is freer to heed the quartet music and develop one's own role in it. Some players will have no time to practice, some will not want to; the more expert may not need to make the effort and may prefer to get their satisfaction out of reading, playing as well as they can.

Perhaps not many quartet groups will have the opportunity, the time, even the interest, to follow out within their own scope the sort of work a professional group must go through. But all quartet players will soon learn, if they do not know it already, that the three principal requirements for ensemble practice are, as Franz Kneisel is said to have remarked, "real reverence, untiring zeal, and punctuality at rehearsals."

This last is indeed to be taken to heart by unprofessional groups. Much time may be wasted, much annoyance bred, by the waiting of three members for a late fourth. Staggered arrivals are hard on those who are ready to begin at an agreed hour.

Not that such time need be altogether lost. One can turn it to profit by practicing three parts together, or even two, especially if the quartet selected is a difficult one. Also there are the string trios to fall back upon (the Mozart *Divertimento*, the Beethoven trios, Dohnányi, Kodály, or, if the cellist is missing, the Dvořák *Terzetto* for two violins and viola). But quartet playing becomes a serious business for those who care enough really to go into it, and if it is only possible to meet once a week or once a fortnight there is always much—delightfully much—to be done.

Every amateur group, like every professional group, will go about rehearsing in its own way and the following paragraphs are meant not as any fixed methods of procedure but merely to offer some suggestions and reminders. They assume a regular foursome of sympathetic individuals, able to put up with each others' idiosyncrasies. The most satisfying results are naturally obtained if the personnel remains the same. The nature of a first meeting will vary with the musical experience of the players, and while its first objective is to get acquainted with the music, it will also bring about the getting acquainted with each other as quartet players and finding out how best to work together.

You have chosen a quartet to start on (perhaps a Haydn, and if you have never played quartet before, perhaps a Haydn minuet movement). You have heard it, you like it, it is not too exacting technically. You are going to read it through. You have tuned. (See pp. 178-79.)

Take a good look at the first page. Note the time signature, the first theme, the second, and whether there are a great many notes on the page, notes of fast values. If there are, register their form—passage, scale, arpeggio—and what keys they seem to go through, so that you are not floored when you come upon them.

Try out a passage in your own part if you must, but *sketch* it, quietly and briefly, for your own benefit only. If all four players start vigorous individual practice at this point, each at the top of his bent, the resulting cacophony simply ruins the atmosphere for making music. Like tuning, these preliminaries should be subdued. The time at your disposal is limited, and it is for ensemble. Perhaps this is hint enough that it *is* a good idea to practice your parts ahead of time.

You exchange views briefly on the tempo, decide to "try it not too fast to begin with." It is safer to go quietly and steadily until you find the right way, which the music will soon enough tell you. And before you actually start to play, *have in mind* what you are going to do with the first measure, the first few measures. Everybody is ready, bow poised close above strings, to begin. The first violin gives the signal (about which more presently, pp. 45-48) and you launch into the adventure.

If the music is familiar you will get further than if you are undertaking something in an unknown style. But as far as you can, keep moving, even if the leader has to count out loud to hold things together; don't give in until you are really making nothing of it. This is not frivolous advice. It is important to *play*, to feel the course of the music so that you will know what to work for. On a first reading you may get through only part of the movement before you would rather go back and start fresh with some understanding of what lies ahead of you. That is good too, but be sure to go through the whole piece. Perhaps you find you have taken it too slowly, then you will pick up the tempo; if too fast, try it slower.

Now it will be time to get to work. How you handle the next stage will depend on what discoveries you have made and what questions these have aroused. Since this little book exists for the purpose of drawing attention to the special musical and technical problems of quartet playing and the substance of all this lies in the following chapters, to be consulted in more detail, let us here just briefly sum up what sort of things to do in rehearsal, how to go about breaking down a movement in order to get at its content.

To start with phrasing. You consider the nature of a phrase. Is it sustained, or flowing, or lively? Bowings and fingerings should be alike; as far as possible, that is, given the characteristics of the different instruments. A phrase may require but a single bow in *piano*, in *forte* two or more, but change of bow should be inconspicuous and not bring with it unintended alterations in the phrasing, as distinguished from intentional alterations of musical significance. The use of up or down strokes at given points is to be considered. The cello often prefers an upbow where the violins would use a down. Whether to use a flat stroke or *spiccato* in a certain passage? Color, register (higher or lower) and dynamic (louder or softer) will help to decide.

On which strings does a phrase or passage sound best? The heavier? The lighter? Is it more effective on one string or is there no harm in crossing to a different timbre? Again, the musical significance should not be interfered with, though fingering is a very individual matter and the best result may be achieved in different ways by different players.

The important thing is that the overall musical result should be consistent, not rigidly, but so as to reflect a unified concept, not everybody fiddling along in his own sweet way. And remember that if your first decisions on these points do not meet the case on further acquaintance with the music, you can always change them for what proves better. These decisions will keep you busy for a long time.

If in difficulties, go over a passage slowly, strictly in

time, measure by measure if need be, as you would in any individual practicing. Work with two voices at a time, then with three, then all four, until you are sure enough to take it up to tempo.

If two instruments encounter a long phrase like that for the violins in Fig. 23—a duet then handed over to viola and cello—they will profit by playing it over together for synchronizing smoothly, for unity of bowing and expression. This holds also for an accompaniment figure that two instruments carry on together (Figs. 102 and 103).

In all you do listen to the intonation too, and you will want to do a little work on that as well (see pp. 176-78). It is remarkable how the texture clears if you are really playing in tune!

While doing all these things you will be thinking more and more closely about the music: about what happens to the themes, the melodic material in its recurrent and varied forms and developments, and what to the relative importance of the voices in bringing out thematic fragments, lending support here, taking over the thread there. The shape and structure of the piece—melodic, harmonic, dynamic—will become your concern. You will consider its proportions, the relative importance of its climaxes: how loud this *forte* should be in relation to the next one, to the nearest *piano*, to an eventual *fortissimo*. You will want to find the most effective use of color in all its varieties. In short, the music will grow under your fingers as its interest grows in your mind. You will pick out little by little what needs most to be done in a next rehearsal.

It may take several meetings to feel you have done sufficient dissecting, that you have broken the back of the piece at least as far as you are able at this point in your acquaintance with it. Then comes the satisfaction of putting it together again. After you have practiced some of the difficult parts, cleared up doubtful places so that they go more smoothly, play it through. More than once. And at your next meeting start by playing it through to see what you have retained of this accomplishment. Then you will find that you can soften the edges, mold the music to satisfying fluency.

Signals

Though the most experienced musician of the group will naturally be the leader, the first violin, even if he is not the most accomplished, should be the one to conduct rehearsals. He should learn to do this because of the nature of his part. He should give the signals, and his colleagues should keep close watch of his doings—"watch" not necessarily with direct glances, but with their quartet player's sixth sense, which might be described as a kind of (mutual) osmotic awareness that never sleeps.

He signals by the slightest dip of his fiddle on the downbeat and a corresponding slightest lift on the up. Better still, when the quartet feels at home with itself, he will use the merest gesture of his head—up, down; even, as when it comes to performance, just a raising of the eyebrows. Just by the natural body-motions in his playing, too, he can convey the flow of the music, the approach to a climax, the restraint of a ritard. But in this he must beware of too much gesturing, must depend rather on his colleagues' familiarity with his intentions, their intuitive awareness.

In rehearsal, then, with the tempo and opening phrase in mind, he leads off with a starting signal. At first he will give a whole measure "for nothing," counting aloud, perhaps, until you are familiar with the music. If he enters on the upbeat of a C or 4/4 measure, he will signal 1-, 2-, 3-, and play on 4. Or in a minuet, he will signal 1-, 2-, and play on 3. If the tempo is slow (as in Fig. 13), he may use the subdivision technique, indicating 1-and, 2-and, and play on 3. In a slow 6/8 it would be enough to give only the 4-, 5- of the second group of eighths, playing on 6. In a fast 6/8, however (as in opening the Mozart B♭, K. 458, the "Hunt"), signaling the groups, 1-, 2-, would establish the tempo for the second violin to enter with him on the last eighth.

The 1-, 2- of the *alla breve* in Fig. 20—down, up—is sufficient to give the cue, since all four enter on the last quarter (the second half of 2-). For the *alla breve* in Fig. 25 he would give the 1-, 2- of an imaginary preceding measure until familiarity would probably render the indication of the imaginary preceding 2- sufficient for the viola to catch the tempo of his triplet figure.

Again, where the tempo is so fast that the measures are counted in *one* only, at least two measures for nothing may be needed in a 4-beat rhythm—down, up—1-, 1-; or in a triple rhythm three—down, up, up—1-, 1-, 1- (Fig. 36).

If another instrument than the first violin starts the movement, or takes the leading voice at a given point, then it is of course up to that player to do the signaling. A good example: the cello's opening of Beethoven's Op. 59, No. 1 (Fig. 22) where he will indicate the imaginary preceding 3-, 4- (later perhaps just the 4- will be enough) with the slightest gesture of his head (or eyebrows), while the second violin and viola are all set to enter exactly on the *one* with him.

Whoever begins, it is imperative for all to be ready, though they may not themselves play for several measures. Everyone must always be *partaking* in the music. Thus the first violin in this same Fig. 22, though he leaves the start to the cello, will in his mind be taking part in the eight measures before he comes in and will through his attentive bearing remain one with his colleagues and convey to the outside world the fact that this is so.

To lead a ritard (the dictionaries do not appear to sanction this word, but we just do not adhere to the formality of "*ritardando*" and speak of a "ritard") it is again by the least emphasis of his playing motions rather than by too marked signals that the first violin holds his companions back with him. How much of a ritard is it? Or is it just that slight natural letting-off of the phrase which is not a ritard? The same, in the opposite sense, with an *accelerando*: he carries them along with his own increasing speed. In the case of a hold ($\frown$), how long to hold it will of course depend on the music; bows must all stop together, come off together, and after that he gives the sign for starting up again.

In ending, as in beginning, one naturally watches the first violin (or whoever has the significant voice at that point) in order to finish exactly together. Is there a ritard? He indicates how much. Is there a final hold? Having found out whether it is to be held in a steady or in a diminishing dynamic, he indicates, perhaps with a slight dip of his fiddle, when to take bows off. If the movement closes with chords, the gesture of his playing signals the attack, so that all four players strike simultaneously. Even after the finish you will find that the current of the music still keeps you together for a moment in such a way as to prevent individual flourishes in taking off bows or too sudden a relapse into relaxed postures.

Once you know the music, there is no problem, and fewer signals are necessary. If there is no upbeat to the opening phrase, for example, the least lift of the first's fiddle is enough to bring all hands together on the *one*. But it must be there! Without it the start is ragged; the first violin must carry out his responsibility or everybody feels uncertain. The more you play together, the better you know each other's ways and the work you are playing, the less obvious should any signals become. One almost hesitates to describe them, indeed, lest words fix them with any implication of rigidity.

Studying the Score

It should be obvious by now how helpful, indeed how necessary, it is to study the score. Familiar music one can find one's way in without difficulty because the lines and harmonies sound in the back of one's mind as one sees them spread out there for the reading. And about an unfamiliar composition—a difficult, a new, a "modern" composition— one can learn a great deal even if one is not so fortunately gifted as to be able to hear in one's head all the strange things that go on. If you are really studying a quartet, blue-pencil the themes, the thematic fragments, the important tone or tones in a harmony: many items, large and small, will come to your notice and you will get a picture of the material, the interplay of the parts, the form, the structure as conveyed by the dynamics as well as by the develop-ments in the content. When you play again, many things will be clearer to you, you will hear better and listen bet-ter and know better what to bring out in molding the music. You will soon find yourself reading a score and enjoying it as you would a book. And even when you are rehearsing familiar music you will want to have a score on hand for reference.

The leader of the quartet is the one who must do most of this studying. The better he "knows the score" the better things go. But every member will feel more at home in the music, will find something that bears on the interest and functions of his own part, will contribute something he has noticed in the score, so that together the group will arrive at a more mellow understanding of the whole as well as of the just proportion of each role.

Uses of Recordings

There are so many good recordings nowadays that an amateur group has an excellent opportunity to become acquainted with quartet works of all sorts. Where the music is familiar one can compare interpretations and find guidance in the details of performance. To listen with score in hand can be delightfully instructive.

Recordings—under the name of "Add-a-Part", "Minus One" and the like—in which one part of a quartet has been left out, are also to be had, so that an individual player can increase his experience by playing along with three invisible colleagues. It is not so easy to play with a record, however, where the living contact with others is lacking and the relentless mechanical course of the music one must join in with allows of no give-and-take—you just have to keep going, whether you sympathize with the interpretation or not.

FOUR

Tempo and Tempo Modification

MUSIC OCCURS IN TIME: tempo is the pulse governing the flow of that time. It binds rhythm and phrase and harmony in continuous progress to a whole. It therefore controls the life of a piece. Mozart considered it the most important element of a musical performance.

A tempo should not be arbitrarily fixed. The composer, hearing two different interpretations of his work, may be definitely satisfied with one or see merit in the sentiment of each; he may even alter his own preconception on listening to the actual performance of the work. But the musician has infrequently the privilege of playing for the composer and he has to fall back on written instructions and perhaps metronomic indications. On a first reading he will be helped by a glance through the score, appraising the likely speed of the *quickest* notes that occur in it, for there is a limit to the speed at which they may be effectively taken; also by noting the *harmonic texture*, for simple harmonies may be more clearly grasped at a rapid passing than complex ones.

These things may give him a hint as to how fast an *Allegro* or how slow an *Adagio* is intended. His final criterion is, in any case, the sense of the theme or phrase in the music itself. Only experiment and *familiarity* with the composition as a whole will give him this and help him determine his tempo. After this, the test of much playing may cause him to alter his interpretation; or he may find that circumstances—such as acoustical effects of different places—affect the distinctness or carrying power of the sound, so that he must be resourceful in handling his tempi to keep his performance up to the mark, whatever the demands made upon it.

The freedom of experimenting may seem on the one hand to leave too much latitude and on the other to give him too little definite assistance in clearing up difficult or less easily understood measures. But here he will find a guide for either case in tradition and in musical style. He knows that the dignified *Allegro* of Bach's day is not necessarily the same as that of a lively last movement of a Haydn quartet; a Mozart *Andantino* or *Allegretto* moves more lightly than a Brahms; there is the slow *Adagio* of the full phrase and large emotion—Beethoven's type—and the more fluent *Adagio* that needs a freer, more elastic treatment—Mozart's type; there are *Vivaces* of every speed—*non troppo, assai, molto*—indications which no metronome ever could convey but which the style of the music does.

This is not to imply any scorn of what one John Harrison, in 1775, called "such a machine as will afford a nice and true mensuration of time." Beethoven wrote that he had long thought of giving up "the nonsensical designations *Allegro, Andante, Adagio, Presto;* Mälzel's metronome gives us the best opportunity to do this." But he said further, "As regards these four speeds, which by no means have the correctness or truthfulness of the chief winds, we gladly allow that they be put aside; it is a different matter with the words used to designate the character of the composition, these we cannot give up, since time is really more the body while these have reference to the spirit." As with the symphonies, in the quartets, for the first eleven of which Beethoven is known to have specified the Mälzel metronomic markings (though the Eulenburg scores, for example, carry over only those for Op. 74 and Op. 95), many different indications stand for the same single Italian term; Beethoven's single terms, too, are more often qualified than not—*con brio, con moto, cantabile, molto, ma non troppo, vivace, scherzoso,* and so forth; and it is not surprising that he should eventually have given up his plan of thus marking all his compositions.

The metronome has its uses, however, not only for defining and establishing a given tempo indication as nearly as possible, but also to keep one going throughout a passage, or a whole movement, in order to find out whether one is really doing what one thinks one is doing. It discloses the weak spots, a sagging here, a rushing there. This is healthy practice for the individual player from time to time, and in the quartet it is astonishing to discover how easily the four together may fall back or run ahead.

For, the tempo once determined, a thousand dangers threaten it in the course of performance: of dragging in slow movements, of running away in fast ones, of unsteadiness when scope is given to the natural demands of expression. The ideal slow tempo would be one that *keeps moving* without losing the slow spirit; the ideal fast tempo, one that keeps steadily brisk *without hastening.*

Sometimes, in working over a piece, one may find that the tempo has lost its original impetus and will need to be revived with a fresh attack. Tempo is not to be mechanically maintained, as by the metronome, which states the single rhythmic unit but proceeds irrespective of the essential subtleties of musical sound. The well-maintained tempo leaves the music all fullness of dynamic variety, all fineness of phrasing—the dilations and contractions of pulsating life—without destroying its continuity, its perfect coherence.

I. A *presto* movement (for example, Fig. 1, below, the last of Haydn's Op. 76, No. 5) starts off in the approved snappy tempo, but presently it seems to have lost vitality, and when the piece is done a not altogether satisfactory impression remains, as of an unsteady enterprise that made port brilliantly enough but only by a sudden last effort. It is possible that, in studying the movement (or in reading, where technical difficulties impede), the slow working-out of passages has bred an irregularity in the whole which may be cured by a brisker, fresher quality throughout, in which such passages will slip quietly into place, clear but inconspicuous. But how to achieve this quality?

Ex. 1: The *prompt inset* of each instrument is most important in maintaining tempo. The first violin should enter on the dot with the theme at (a), and the cello likewise (in the last bar quoted here):

Fig. 1

The instruments which carry the accompaniment over blank spaces between the melodies are responsible for the immediate re-announcement of the tempo (second violin and viola at [c]). The only guarantee of a prompt inset is *to have the bow ready to drop on the string.* Each player is part of a whole that is already under way, continuously going, and the fraction of time it takes to start his voice may already make his entrance *sound too late.* The expert quartet player is forehanded: with his bow near or on the string he starts his tone almost *before* the beat, so that it sounds *on* the beat and no precious instant is lost in preliminary motions (see also p. 62, to Fig. 9).

Ex. 2: Immediate *picking-up* of the tempo is necessary after places that, for their musical value, demand a slight broadening. In Fig. 2 the *forte* needs to be definitely established by the slightest broadening of the first couple of high sixteenths, but the return to the absolute tempo must then be accomplished in the space of the very next eighth, so that the third and fourth eighths of the measure may be as lively as ever:

Fig. 2

Shortly after this, the first half of the movement closes, and there is an interlude finishing in a descending unison in the chord of Bb, *forte,* upon which the middle voices restate the accompaniment to the theme. This is their op-

portunity to check up on the general bearing of the tempo
and give it fresh impetus.

Fig. 3

Ex. 3: The reverse is also true. In Fig. 4 the unison,
crescendo, tends to a slight increase in speed; the accented
half-notes, however, may need to be *held back* for emphasis. Therefore, at the *piano,* the tempo should be immediately restored:

Fig. 4

Ex. 4: A rapid theme, if at all unsteady, is liable to sound as though the notes were falling over each other. The only salvation is in observing the *full value* of each note and group, testing them to be sure no notes are slighted. This does not mean that such a theme (Fig. 1) should be reduced to sounding mechanical. Its *natural action* should remain unimpaired, the two sixteenths belonging to, and heading toward, the following eighth. If bowed as indicated, the proper effect is more easily preserved.

It is often helpful, where rapid notes of various denominations occur interwoven through all the voices—sixteenths against dotted eighths or syncopations, etc.—to practice such passages first slowly, then up to tempo, *all in the smallest denomination* (cf. p. 38). Exact values and rhythmic relations are thus established and a clear and steady ensemble made possible. Here, too, the very slight accenting of the first of a group of notes helps the steadiness.

II. In slow movements, some quartets incline to very slow tempi, others to slightly faster, but the essential spirit is to be preserved in the one case without dragging, in the other without unsteadiness. An *Adagio* like that of Mozart's Quartet in D (K. 499, Fig. 5) requires positive liberty of handling, but all within the meaning of an *adagio*, within the frame of the measured tempo.

Ex. 1: As in the *Presto* just discussed (Fig. 1), it is important to observe full value in all melody tones and in melodious bridging fragments in order to give breadth to the music. The importance may then be well grasped of observing *accuracy* in the *comparative values* of the small notes, sixteenths or thirty-seconds. A casual reading or careless playing does not reach into the innate interest of the opening theme nor achieve the singing beauty that is characteristic of it:

Fig. 5

Ex. 2: Although the thematic group of four sixteenths which is characteristic throughout this movement (Fig. 6, last measure) should not be hurried or made unsteady, it becomes very monotonous if, in preserving their full value, the two separated sixteenths are always played *all alike broad*. Variety may be given by playing some shorter, more *slightly*, though still rhythmically. Where these notes are of harmonic significance they should of course be broad, but where they are not, they may be treated as suggested.

Ex. 3: Harmonic sequences, if taken too literally in tempo, seem to impede the movement forward of the music. They demand a gradual, *subdued acceleration* or fluency, which may be resorted to without hurry. They should remain calm, since restlessness or excitement would destroy the *adagio* spirit, and should broaden again into the original sustained tempo as soon as the monotony has been relieved. In the following example, the three other voices easily follow the freedom of the first violin, helping to keep the tempo broad by the *slightest tenuto* on the first sixteenth of each group, no more than the least emphasis on the crowning *forte*:

Fig. 6

Ex. 4: The first violin's thirty-second-note passages in Fig. 7, below, are practically *cadenzas* and as such need variety and grace. Freedom is again legitimate here, since it makes up for the fragment of motion lost at the start of the first group by the necessary little break or pause for clarity (between *forte* and *piano*, see under Dynamics, p. 100, The Pause or Lift) and the slight delay marking the change from *f* to *p* in the *fp*; and this freedom should be promptly paid back by moving with the cello's steady eighths and by the natural broadening of the *crescendo*-to-*forte* finish of the phrase:

Fig. 7

III. Any movement, then, as it passes through thematic evolutions and entanglements, is liable to lapse in some manner from its original freshness of tempo. Music of the romantic type, and especially certain modern music with its inclination to be fragmentary and its dependence on *treatment* for effect, requires an *exaggerated degree of give-and-take,* a highly alert sense for the *constant resumption* of tempo. This is also true of both the Debussy and the Ravel quartets. In the opening of the latter especially, give-and-take is needed *phrase by phrase*: that is, each phrase must run clearly and freely to its full expression; therefore each subsequent phrase must *pay back*, by prompt entrance with the original characteristic tempo, any liberties allowed its predecessor.

IV. Accompaniments, instead of providing a background of support, often influence the tempo adversely. The monotony of a repeated figure or series of repeated notes can hypnotize the player until he does not fully control the motions of his bow and fingers and his work becomes irregular, falls behind the music it is supposed to be assisting or hurries ahead of it. Passages of this sort should be critically watched. A good accompaniment is one that remains always *alive to what it accompanies* (for example, Fig. 11).

V. It is customary to speak of "feeling" a tempo; studious counting alone does not always produce the spirit, though it may control the performance, of the movement forward. This is illustrated in the difference between feeling a long measure of 6, 9, or 12 eighths *in eighths* and feeling it in the rhythmically correct sense of its important beats, 2, 3, or 4 (as has been mentioned under Counting). In the following measures from the *Adagio* of Beethoven's Op. 18, No. 1, the movement forward would be altogether lost during the long pauses if counted in eighths, whereas feeling three beats, and each third beat as leading over into the first of the next measure, supports the tempo so that the pauses do not sound like gaps. The drawing of the bows is important here, for while they should remain on the string only for the given quarter-note, they should leave the sort of long resonance that seems to linger in the ear during the silences (see also p. 136, Ex. 3):

Fig. 8

(Adagio)

VI. The handling of tempo suggested in sections I, II, and III implies a most *delicately manipulated give-and-take* far more subtle than any actual *ritard* or *accelerando* or even *rubato*. These last are all more powerful, are part of the musical dynamic and, save for the *rubato*, which is usually left to the players, are indicated by the composer. *Rubato*, as generally understood, is a purposely free treatment, whether gentle or passionate in mood. It is a more fluent or a bolder liberty of phrasing than the delicate manipulation under discussion, which, while based on phrasing (the natural demands of expression), should be so fine as to remain as a means practically unnoticeable. It has been called "the triumph and the danger of the virtuoso," who uses the *rubato* when and as he pleases in his understanding of the music—one has but to recall Casals playing Bach for an unsurpassed example of musicianship in this respect. Debussy gives the indication: "*à tempo rubato*"; Ravel, instead, practically writes out the effects he wants by means of numerous instructions: *accel.*, *cédez*, *pressez*, *poco rit.*, and so on, though it may be assumed that within his elastic phrases he does not intend too obvious a degree of freedom. In short, the *rubato* should be circumspectly used in accordance with the style of the music. In the treatment of a recurrent phrase this will allow for the characteristic expressive quality of the individual instrument to whose turn it falls, without each player's pulling it about too freely in his own way.

None of these suggestions for broadening or easing off the tempo or preserving the movement forward implies so much as even a slight *ritard* or *accelerando*. The true *ritard* is practically always marked, even in the earlier quartets, and has rarely to be introduced by the interpreter. Its degree and extent—whether great or slight, gradual or sudden—is determined (unless indicated) by the *sense and style of the music* alone. Beethoven writes a whole quartet (Op. 18, No. 1) without a single *ritard*, while one movement of some modern quartet may contain a dozen *ritards* and *accelerandos* of different degrees, besides actual tempo changes. Beethoven practically replaces these means by his remarkable use of dynamics, and this should make one all the more wary in handling his tempos. In the following measures (Op. 18, No. 1):

(Allegro con brio)

Fig. 9

there may be a tendency for the first violin to slow up on the *pianissimo* echo of the second violin's sixth extending the original motive. But if this tendency is humored, the second violin involuntarily repeats its motive a little slower, whereupon the second echo by the first violin comes out slower yet—in fact, the whole phrase makes a *ritard*, which was evidently not Beethoven's intention. If the first violin has his bow *near the string*, his entrance will be punctual, the second violin can repeat his figure in tempo, and there will be no hanging on to the final *pp* to spoil the effect of the surprise *forte* entrance of the cello.

VII. When an actual change of tempo is called for within a movement—whether or no there is a metronomic indication, and these are not always infallible—it will usually be found that a clear relation holds between the new tempo and the old. Where, for instance, the *Adagio cantabile* of Op. 18, No. 2, quoted in Fig. 13 (Beethoven's music is full of such examples), goes over into the central *Allegro* section in 2/4, the quarter-note of the latter simply has half the value of the former quarter, that is, moves twice as fast. This is very prettily prepared by the composer through the four-sixteenths figures in the closing bars of the 3/4 which then become the thematic motive of the 2/4, while the shorter measure adds to the effect of a livelier speed. Or, again, in the third movement of Op. 127, the five *Allegro* measures in 2/4 would keep the same quarter-note beat as the *Scherzando vivace*, whereas the *Presto* section would fit in at one bar to that beat or three times as fast.

It is well, in reading, to look over the music first for any such tempo changes; then one will not be caught unaware, or make a difficulty of deciding how the new tempo is to be taken.

FIVE

Phrasing

THE NEED FOR HOMOGENEOUS PHRASING throughout the four voices of a quartet has been mentioned. A solitary player may improvise any effect he pleases on the inspiration of a moment, but since a theme or figure is likely to occur in whole or in part through all the quartet's voices, its interpretation should be worked out as uniformly as possible. The resulting conformity will not be hard-and-fast or monotonous. It will be subject to many considerations: of color, register, texture, the technical delivery of the different instruments, the varying significance of the phrase in the composition: but the understanding remains the same. Phrasing, which must be clear in any solo work, has added demands made upon it in quartet playing. The four voices must fit together to produce much more complicated music with the same distinctness; they must articulate what they are doing so that it carries clearly to the hearing distance of an audience. A foundation of clear phrasing is essential to developing the dynamics and color of quartet music.

I. Each phrase or figure should be *well finished* in itself, not only for musical clarity and carrying power, but also so that it may be used, molded, adjusted to best advantage in its recurrences and developments. It is then easily woven through the harmonic and textural complexes of the music and is easily recognizable through them. Thus, too, it is possible to throw a passage or a detail *into relief*, giving plasticity to the music, modeling, variety.

Ex. 1: To effect this finish an *imperceptible wait* (frequently referred to by its German name, *Luftpause*) is often necessary, to let the resonance of one phrase or figure die out and to mark the beginning of the next, so that the ear may be prepared to take in the new matter. The following phrases (first movement of the Mozart D Major, K. 499) need to be presented thus distinctly. The imperceptible wait (marked by the comma) is important in the first violin, which closes one phrase and begins another, and especially so in the second violin, which here finishes one phrase as a secondary voice and starts the next as leading voice:

(Allegretto)

Fig. 10

Depending on the tempo and type of the theme, this effect is very often achieved by merely shortening a little the last note of the first phrase. In this particular instance, however, it is important not to cut the D short: as top tone of a highly resonant tonic chord-line it is liable to stick out louder than its function warrants and, if shortened, to sound jerky, and moreover in the theme itself there is a definite distinction between eighth-note and quarter-note values to be observed. It is instructive to note that the first time this passage occurs in the movement (at measure 16) it is the viola that takes over the restatement, so that for the second violin the problem does not arise here of distinguishing between two phrases.

Ex. 2: The accompanying voices of the violins (Haydn, Op. 76, No. 5) should assist the finish of the viola's solo and the start of the cello's by *slightly indicating* such a wait—really no more than a coming-in-afresh with the cello, instead of continuing their repeated eighths in humdrum fashion over the instant of the change:

Fig. 11

(Largo, cantabile e mesto)

Ex. 3: The *incisive inset*, so useful in maintaining tempo, is also a help in defining phrase-groups. It is indispensable in projecting tones so that they carry immediately to a distance; also in making sure the voice leading is intelligible. In the following passage (Mozart, K. 499) the viola's insistent E is an important note, entering alone as it does, and while in the *forte* it is easily enough heard, its *piano* entrances are lost unless their inset is distinct:

Fig. 12

(Allegretto)

Ex. 4: A phrase may need to be finished by *dropping the tone,* not retarding but diminishing the volume at the rest-point of the cadence. In the sixth measure of Beethoven's slow melody (Op. 18, No. 2) the first violin's closing C would be eased off in this way (it is only an eighth, and it needs no emphasis since the cello's C establishes the tonic chord) so that the sound may die away before the melody resumes with its upbeat on the same C. The viola's 32nd-notes (like its F# in the third measure) should come clearly through the held tones of the others, the E being allowed to die away with the rest of the chord:

Fig. 13

In the third measure of the same phrase this letting-off would naturally be less marked, this being only a semi-cadence on the dominant, the resonance of which leads over to the continuation of the melody on the eighth-note dominant-seventh, F. Note that this *is* an eighth-note upbeat, not a quarter as at the beginning.

Ex. 5: Where one phrase-group or sequence rapidly succeeds another the final note of the first may need to be docked of a little of its written length lest, if held literally, it sounds ponderous or obscures the next entrance. This—not a detachment—is surely the meaning of the dot under the

third beats in the second and fourth measures of the opening phrase of Beethoven's Op. 18, No. 4:

Fig. 14

II. Distinct and unhesitant *voice leading* is one foundation of clear phrasing. It goes without saying that each
voice as it has the melody or an important thematic figure
should be heard above the others. But it requires some care
and skill to bestow the right emphasis on *fragments*—sometimes no more than a couple of notes, or even a single tone
in an inner voice—which are momentarily of melodic or
harmonic import yet should be not unduly conspicuous but
always quietly interwoven with the other voices. In studying a score it is a great help to blue-pencil such fragments
throughout, clarifying to the eye the structural details and
so having a definite picture in mind of what to listen for in
playing.

Ex. 1: Throughout the opening phrase of the *Adagio* of
Beethoven's Op. 74 (the "Harp") the melodious fragments
of the lower voices must be heard in the undercurrent
mezza voce to the high melody of the first violin: the chromatic progressions for the sake of harmonic distinction, the
sixteenth-note figures because they are characteristic, the

frequent sixths and thirds for the melodious nature of their
contribution to the harmony:

Fig. 15

The three lower parts, indeed, are almost complete in
themselves, an illustration of the equal value of all four
voices in the quartet texture. This example also suggests
another point, namely, that not always *every* note in a
group is equally important. In the second measure, for
instance, the viola's first two notes, Eb–E, should be
brought out, whereas the following, F–Eb are secondary to
the melody-tones, Db–C, of the violin.

Ex. 2: A few notes (sometimes only a single tone) *leading to a resolution* may have to be brought out with what
at first seems exaggerated strength in order to clear the sense
of the phrase. So with the viola's part in the Haydn D
Major, Op. 76, No. 5:

Fig. 16

Ex. 3: Where two voices overlap, one finishing, the other beginning, a phrase, the former should yield to let the entrance of the latter be heard. In the following example (Mozart D Major, K. 575, first movement) the first violin's final A is not so important as the entering A of the second violin and should be dropped to almost nothing:

Fig. 17

Ex. 4: The late quartets of Beethoven offer astonishing examples of voice leading, passages that require careful study and painstaking execution, though they sound entirely innocent. The interesting thematic matter in the measures quoted below (from the *Andante con moto, ma non troppo—poco scherzoso* of Op. 130) may be picked out as in a puzzle. In the first measure cello and viola have the thematic eighths, of which only the first two are important, the cello's Db yielding to the viola's as the viola completes the ascending line Bb–C–Db–Eb. In the next measure the thematic sixteenths and the *tenuto* quarters are to be picked out, this same line occurring in reverse in the first violin, Eb–Db–C–Bb. In the third measure this line is traced once more, the first violin's Eb, cello's Db and C, second violin's C and Bb, so that the cello's first Db is more important than its last and than the second violin's first

Bb, while the second's last Bb is more important than its first and than the cello's last Db:

(Andante con moto ma non troppo)

Fig. 18

III. The phrase-line is highly susceptible to the mechanics of tone-production, to the uses of register, string, finger, bow. Involuntarily quite perverse effects may occur. A high note may strike a shrill spot, a low one be so resonant that it is too loud; also an instrument may speak better in one register or on one string than another. One must consider the emphasis that falls on certain tones, whether it is natural and justified or accidental and contrary to the musical intention. Unless the composer's purpose is specifically evident, such points must pass the judgment of a sensitive ear.

Ex. 1: In this "very expressive" Ravel melody everything tends to emphasize the Bb. It is the lowest tone in the phrase; it coincides with a change of direction and of bow; it is the fourth scale-step, approached by a whole-tone progression and having a stronger tendency to move down than up; it falls on the second accented beat of the measure, and two instruments are playing it in unison a resonant two octaves apart. It seems to gather too much tone to itself and push out of the flowing *pianissimo* character of the phrase. Therefore it needs to be handled gently (see p. 75, Ex. 1):

Allegro moderato

Fig. 19

The above excerpt from Quartet by Ravel used by permission of A. Durand & Cie., Paris, France.

Ex. 2: The opening phrase of the Mozart (K. 499) already cited (Fig. 10) presents a problem of *counteracting a natural accent*. The first and third quarters of the first measure are written as an eighth followed by an eighth rest: evidently Mozart wanted to avoid for his theme the natural weight that would fall on those accented beats. But even as written, played short, these eighths are liable to sound accented or jerky. How to avoid this? By *thinking* slightly more emphasis on the preceding quarter which, being on a weak beat, needs to be presented with a little added conviction to make it tell, give it a singing quality which it hands over to the eighth-note. In this instance the opening F♯ is hardly an upbeat. It is itself the start of the

theme, and from it Mozart derives the little figure ♪♫
with which he plays throughout the piece, varying it to
♫♪ and even reversing its rhythm to ♫♪. The problem
of emphasis continues through the whole phrase, for now
the low unison tones, first repeated (♩♩♩♩) and then
held (♩.) may sound heavy, like a dull interruption to
the melody's flow. But this will not be the case if the quarters are kept light and lively and the held tones quietly
vibrant, while the little characteristic figure tossed back
and forth on the off beats is brought out:

Allegretto

Fig. 20

Many such problems come up in working out one's understanding of a composition. They are endlessly varied
and challenging. Style, tradition, musical custom and taste
offer help in solving them. But it is in the freshness of his

own contribution that the quartet player keeps his work alive, finding reward in the enjoyment of discovery.

Bowing

Identity of bowing, wherever possible, is one of the requirements of good ensemble. Not only that divisions of the bow, slurs, staccatos, legatos should sound homogeneously throughout the four voices; nor because of the aesthetic effect on the listener, who is also a watcher and to be agreeably influenced by harmonious motion and disturbed by inconsistent, contrary, disconnected lines. Ensemble, and especially the quartet, teaches the full significance of the bow in phrasing. Up-strokes and down-strokes have different values; insets and finishes also. These affect both the production of tone and the style of the playing. It is necessary to dwell somewhat insistently on these points, which are perhaps no more than inherent in any good bowed-instrument technique, because the delicate balance of the quartet's four-voice structure is sensitive to inconsistencies.

The qualification of "wherever possible" is needed for several reasons. Whether all four bows are actually drawn with the same stroke depends on differences in the instruments and on the effect to be produced. The violins as a rule would be expected to bow alike, the viola, being the same type of instrument, usually with them. The cello, on the other hand, may have to use an opposite stroke to produce the same sort of tone. Circumstances also may require dissimilar bowings for better effect: register, volume of sound, convenience. But generally speaking, similarity is to be desired.

I. The *amount of bow* and the *sort of stroke* used have considerable bearing on the manipulation of the phrase.

Ex. 1: In the Ravel melody (Fig. 19) the troublesome Bb can be controlled and its prominence checked, more

especially since the voices playing it are doubled, by drawing less bow than one has a tendency to draw. Similarly,
one can avoid pushing the triplets following the long E's by
taking only so much bow for the long notes that the return
stroke provides enough and *not too much* bow for them.

Ex. 2: Often notes that fall on an unaccented beat, especially little notes naturally taken up-bow, are neglected
to the detriment of the phrasing. They will come into their
own simply by reversing the strokes and taking them down-
bow, thus removing one of the natural obstacles against
which they were trying to sound. Of such a nature is the
characteristic ♪♪ in Fig. 10. In the up-bow it sounds weak,
partly because the following quarter-note on the accented
beat is reinforced by a down-bow which it does not need.
The little figure acquires a fairer emphasis taken down-
bow, leaving the lightness of the up-bow for the quarter-
note.

Of a somewhat similar nature is the following figure
(Haydn, Op. 64, No. 3) which may be converted from an
awkward motion to one piquant and elegant in character
merely by taking the eighth-note lightly in up-bow and the
16ths down-bow, with the little natural skip that comes
when the bow is dropped on the string (just above the
middle, bow drawn very lightly, lifted no higher than
necessary):

(Vivace assai)

Fig. 21

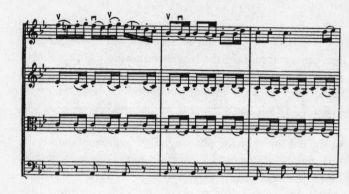

II. A *smooth bow*, in which the changes are not noticeable, belongs to a good violin technique. Where four voices are combined and every defect is so much the more apparent, it is of the greatest importance in the articulation of phrasing.

Ex. 1: No bowing could be too smooth for the following theme of Beethoven's Op. 59, No. 1 (the first "Rasoumovsky") where bar-lines are a mere convention and can be thought away:

Fig. 22

and again in the duets elaborating upon it:

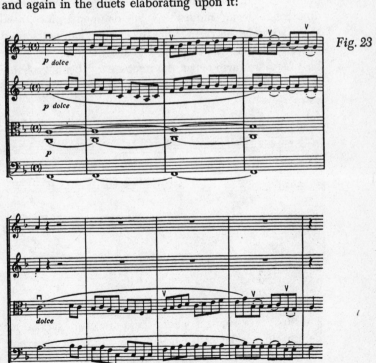

Fig. 23

III.   There are also phrases, however, in which the *change of bow* indicates rhythmic accents or thematic groupings and has therefore a musical purpose. It should always be borne in mind that distance may require exaggeration: that there are effects which sound clear to the player himself or to his colleagues as well but are lost outside a very small radius. Hence the importance of detail in quartet practice; hence also the importance to acoustical clarity of so tiny an action as a change of bow.

Ex. 1: There is no written or intended accent as such on the two half-notes in these *forte* measures (Mozart, K. 499) but if played ahead without special attention the phrase is flat and meaningless. The three introductory quarters, following suddenly as they do upon a *piano,* need to be strongly delivered, after which the half-notes must be very marked, attacked even to the point of lifting the bow between them to get the inset clear (this is probably the meaning of the editorial dots over these notes in the score):

Fig. 24

Ex. 2: Brahms insisted very much upon the importance of distinct bow-changes where these are characteristic for the phrasing. In his own music they are to be heeded most particularly. Just as, when he intends a *legato* he marks a slur sometimes including several measures (more than can

be taken in one bow, hence the change to be imperceptible), so by his shorter slurs he indicates intentional grouping of notes to be distinctly executed. The opening measures of the A Minor Quartet at once take on more character if, without interrupting the flowing progress of the melody, the entry of the D (3rd measure) is heard, and again that of the C and A (9th and 11th measures) which do not belong to the preceding measures but start fresh after the

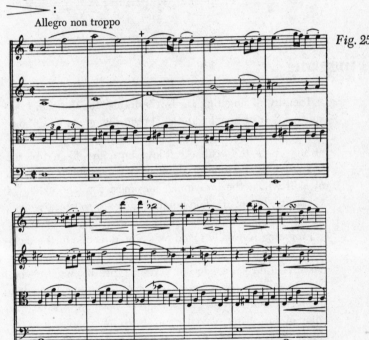

Fig. 25

Again, four measures later, there should be a slight lift of the bow to point the inset of each syncopated note (and especially at +) in contrast to the subsequent real, and unsyncopated, legato cadence: *

* These examples Brahms pointed out to the Kneisel Quartet, who rehearsed the work with him.

Fig. 26

Fingering

Identity of fingering is also desirable, for the same reasons as that of bowing and again with its given exceptions. Here too the rise and fall of the phrase-line, the prominence of high-spots, the weakness of low-spots, are affected by the technique of the tone production. It is not only a question of skill which the individual may master to the extent of virtuosity, but of the fine points which are so sensitive in a quartet because four must play with the fineness of one.

Fingering is usually taken for granted as one of the technical concerns of the solo instrument, so that the player has a routine knowledge of certain types of fingering before he ever comes to do quartet work. He now finds new problems, delicate ones. A change of position, a slide, the color of the string played upon, have new and more considerable consequences. Every technical motion must be subdued, unnoticeable. One may not play a brilliant technical passage in the same manner as alone because it is involved with the other parts playing at the same time. To be a brilliant quartettist is another matter than being a brilliant soloist, and the one does not necessarily succeed in the role of the other.

The type of fingering required in quartet playing is that which will do the most with the least effort. Certain general principles may be set down:

(a) Staying in the position as much as possible, reaching up and down: in other words, extending the range of the hand.

(b) Generally speaking, as little shifting as possible, and always with the utmost smoothness and rapidity of motion.

(c) Attention to changes of string according to the color and quality of tone desired, and also in relation to combinations with the strings of the other instruments. It will frequently be found that the tone of the first position, often avoided by soloists as less expressive than that of higher positions on a lower string, sounds better than the latter in combining with the other instruments and in producing clear harmonies.

Once again it seems almost supererogatory to list these factors which would appear to be no more than any good fiddling would include. It is in the manner of their use that they will be influenced by quartet style. That style should affect the players' technique, not be affected by it.

There is no way of determining any given fingering for any given passage. Individuals will differ in their choice of fingerings: personal idiosyncrasies, preferences natural to the conformation of a hand, the response of the instrument, all go into the player's experience to guide his decisions. One will find more strength in his third finger than in his fourth in high passages, jumps or reaches; another will feel a more satisfactory vibration in a certain position with his second finger than with his third, or vice versa. Joachim was never satisfied with a stated way of doing things and experimented freely with fingerings and bowings, often to the embarrassment of his colleagues. It is true that sometimes a fingering decided on during practice does not prove out in performance and must be revised. But to change an accustomed fingering just before performance is hazardous; habit is apt to assert itself, to the confusion of the player.

The Slide

Individual peculiarities are undoubtedly to be taken into account in choosing the best way of giving value to the important tones of a phrase. But here one of the first and most important points we come up against is the effect on the phrase-line of the motions of *shifting* or of *sliding*. The Ravel melody of Fig. 19 illustrates a problem in fingering as well as in bowing. We have seen that anything that makes the B♭ conspicuous is to be avoided. Therefore it would be well to avoid shifting to it, since the motion of the change would bring it to the fore even if smoothly done. The shift will have to be made in a less conspicuous spot.

The use of the *slide* becomes dangerous in quartet music. The effect should be considered from several angles: the style of the music, whether a slide is really needed, whether it should be a heavy, passionate kind of slide or a light, quick one, scarcely audible yet giving warmth to the phrase. But first of all the fact should be envisaged that any principal phrase launched, say, by the first violin with great expression, is likely to recur at one time or another and in one form or another in every voice, and that a distinct slide, suitable for a solo voice, can become appalling when repeated over and over again.

"There's a train at four-four," said Miss Jenny,
"Four tickets I'll take, have you any?"
"Not four for four-four,"
Said the man at the door,
"For four for four-four is too many."

The individual player must therefore be prepared to sacrifice his particular warm slide if everyone's sliding afflicts the music with a sentimental yowling; or to leave the privilege to that instrument in whose part, and in that part of the piece played, it may be appropriate. One is tempted to say: in quartet playing *never slide*, because of the shocking impurities that technical act may produce in this purest of music. But then one thinks of Hungarian and other folk music in which certain slides are typical and significant.* Therefore it may be better to say that the slide should only be used when it is *characteristic*—and even then with reservations.

This is a matter not of individual taste but of quartet style, of phrase values. The slide attracts attention to the tone slid to. The legitimate slide—like the singer's *portamento*—is one that correctly emphasizes the relative values of tones in a phrase, giving warmth to an important progression. The slide to beware of (one much heard, alas, in certain types of violin playing) is the sort done out of ignorance in places which do not need, and so should not have, the additional emphasis in the phrase-line. This sort of slide robs the legitimate slide of its effectiveness and spoils the real expressiveness of the music. It seems to become a habit with some players; they let it be heard with every interval that goes out of one position. They do not seem to be aware that it is for the most part a technical carelessness or sluggishness, a defective shifting. It is an easy habit to fall into and, like most habits, functions without thought. It shows a lack of critical listening by the player, and a lack of artistic refinement, since he does not distinguish between a musical effect and a mechnical act.

* Bartók, again, calls for a strong slide of an octave, or more or less, both up and down, and sometimes even indicates that an intermediate note should be heard. But these may be looked upon as *effects* rather than as the sort of expressive gesture within a phrase under discussion here.

Let us suppose three notes on the A string: If the B is the important tone in the group, slide to it from the F#, by all means, but then do not slide up from it again to the G. If the G is the important tone, slide up to it from the B, but then do not slide to the B beforehand from the F#, a slide for which there would be no need and which would spoil the emphasis on the G; this move should be accomplished by a rapid and inaudible shift. Beware in any case of that defective shifting which lets an actual tone be heard between the two notes in question because the sliding finger does not quit the string in time on the way down or is slow to give over to the high note on the way up—as, in our example, the third finger letting the D be heard as it gets down to the first position, or the first finger lingering an instant on the third position D on its way up to the 4th finger's G. This, of course, is bad playing in any music.

Of course it is not always necessary to abstain from the brief slide of a single step up or down, save in so far as it may distort the phrase-values of the notes involved. It is naturally a very useful method of proceeding up and down the string and of injecting extra warmth into the expression. It is well, however, to refrain from sliding to a note that is too brief or for some other reason unable to bear the emphasis without sounding disproportionately loud; or, if such a shift is unavoidable, it should at least be as inconspicuous as possible.

As a check to undue sliding it is useful to remember that expression is not enhanced by the slide alone; quality and warmth must first be in the tones themselves; the slide is a secondary effect. In the case of a unison of two voices there may be times when both will slide, but more often it is enough if one does, and that one will be the warmer in tone or color, the leading voice of the moment, to whom the other will yield a little.

These considerations on the slide apply particularly to the "pure" style of the classics. But they are just as much to be pondered in the performance of all other types of composition, not as hard-and-fast rules but because they stem from the characteristic groundwork of quartet style which underlies all quartet music, classical, romantic, or modern, and which without refinement comes to nothing.

SIX

Dynamics

THE CONVENTIONAL DYNAMIC MARKS—*p*, *pp*, *mf*, *f*, *ff*, *cre-scendo*, *diminuendo*, etc.—have come in for every sort of criticism as inadequate to convey the composer's exact idea of *how* soft or *how* loud he conceives a passage to be. Any effort to express intentions more accurately would be welcome. But descriptive phrases do not get much nearer their objective than the accepted Italian expressions of which they are for the most part merely translations into a more familiar language. The real difficulty is that *dynamics are purely relative*: relative not only to each other but to the whole music of which they are an element. The only possible criterion for them, inside the frame of the conventions, is that which the music itself provides.

Quartet style demands that dynamics be made the most of. This is to be done not in mere extremes of contrast, which may be no more than grotesque, but with due regard to the intrinsic interest of the music and in accord with its character and its style. Brilliant contrasts may be called for or only subdued changes. A *forte* in Brahms, moreover, may be differently read from one in Mozart. Or in a single work there may be half a dozen varieties of *forte*, of *piano*, of *pianissimo*, according to the significance of the passage in question in relation to its surroundings and to the structure of the movement as a whole. The term *poco forte* is often misread as a degree in *forte*, but as a rule it occurs in a dynamic setting not of *forte* but of *piano*, for which reason it may be taken to mean something on the order of the old Italian indication *piano ma con suono—piano* but with sound or tone—in other words, sounding out a little more than the surrounding dynamic degree. Fig. 18 illustrates the sort of problem that arises in this connection. The *pp—cresc.—poco f* appear to be introductory degrees to the consistently *mf tenuto* quarter-note (see Fig. 18 and reference to the phrasing of this passage).

Much early quartet music, of which there is a great mass that is valued chiefly as a record, since it has for obvious reasons fallen by the wayside, has no dynamic indications save a formal *f* and *p*. But as the music becomes intrinsically more interesting the number and variety of expression marks increase until dynamics become established as quite as much a part of the music as the notes themselves.

Comparison of a solo or an orchestral score with a quartet score shows how vastly more complex dynamics can be in this last. This is not unreasonable, since the orchestra is too large a tone-mass to be as easily wielded, and the solo player has the greater freedom of his individual interpretation, while the quartet, that highly refined combination of four stringed instruments, permits of more subtlety than the one and more variety than the other, which must, however, be worked out with a keen sense of relative values throughout its texture.

This comparison holds for Beethoven's own works (though the later Piano Sonatas of course resemble the late Quartets, both being fruits of the great period in which his thought molded any medium into freer shapes than it had ever taken before). An examination of his use of dynamics in the Quartets is indeed a most instructive study. It shows quartet players the infinite variety of effects and the vital importance of working them out, of rendering them effectively. It also suggests to the composer extraordinary possibilities in the intensification of expression which are still far from exhausted today.

We have it that Beethoven was extremely meticulous about his markings; therefore we may trust to a good edition * of the Quartets as less subject to editorial idiosyncrasies than is the case with many works of earlier composers. We are quickly aware of certain characteristic means like the *crescendo* leading, surprisingly, to a *piano*: ◁ *p*. (See Fig. 43). We also have it from experience and tradition that his written *crescendo* or *diminuendo* meant a more important rise or fall than the "hairpin" marks ◁ ▷. Any excerpt from the last Quartets will illustrate his idea of dynamic meaning. Take that in Fig. 18, or this from the *Adagio* of Op. 127:

Fig. 27

* The Breitkopf and Härtel edition is perhaps to be recommended; in the early Peters (edited by Joachim & Moser) one should allow

They are stirring problems, these last Quartets, even for the experienced player who has given them long and reverent study. Measures like these have to be gone over in segments, and a whole movement in turn measure by measure, before the full value and accurate performance of these passages becomes clear and understood, before the whole can be reconstructed and construed from its larger meaning. Here dynamics are indeed part and parcel of the musical thought. Modest players are shy before these Quartets, hesitating to approach them. And rightly so, though not to the extent of never getting acquainted with them at all. Surely great works of art are the best models to work from. So much can be learned that one can apply to simpler problems. This is not mere turning to the past with conservative hindsight. It is appreciation that learning from the greatest things that have yet been is a sound preparation for future achievements.

A definition is called for. What do we mean by the question of dynamics? And how can it be separated from that of color? We shall here try to consider dynamics as the element in expressiveness affecting the current of music, the intensification or diminution in volume or speed of its progress. Color, on the other hand, we differentiate as, figuratively speaking, the relatively more static element of quality, of tonal variety and the refinements of four-voice texture. The two are almost inseparable, and they are constantly interactive, often one and the same. Color, understood in the general sense of the variety and interest of a work, includes dynamics. But for purposes of analysis and in order to achieve more thinking about quartet style, it is worthwhile to distinguish between them and get at the essence of each wherever possible.

---

for interpretations being Moser's rather than Joachim's, to judge from the latter's reluctance to set down fingerings and bowings.

Gradations

Obviously the first problem in handling dynamics is a proper distinction between *pianos* and *fortes* and all the midway degrees of loud and soft that lie between. The strength of any one of these will always depend on what precedes and what follows it. We have seen that these marks are purely relative. First and last, the piece as a whole has to be considered, its thematic material, its climaxes and their structural significance, but there is a process of intermediate detail to be gone through concerning each of these in its component parts and in relation to the surrounding material. Here it becomes evident whether the *piano* is a louder or a softer one, the *mezzoforte* nearer the degree of *piano* or of *forte*, the *forte* large and heroic or merely stronger than what went before. Here also the extent of the *crescendo* is to be determined, whether it is the only *crescendo* within a certain section and therefore most important, or whether it is one of several, and if so, whether these several progress cumulatively or are independent of one another. There is an endless variety of varieties. There is no rule for them save only the rule for all dynamics: *consider them well in order to intensify the expression and keep the interest of the music alive.*

I. If a dynamic degree is prolonged over a considerable space it runs two risks: first, of *flagging* in itself, and second, of growing *monotonous* to the listener. The first difficulty may be overcome by understanding how to *sustain* the dynamic degree, the second by discovering in what manner variety may be worked into it without being apparent.

Ex. 1: A passage like the following (from the first movement of Beethoven, Op. 18, No. 1), if it suffers in the first respect will also be suffering from indecision. It should be easy enough to sustain the *forte* and with interest, since there is constant opportunity for fresh insets. Each entrance should be made with an equally vigorous *forte* and equally new spirit, the dotted quarters giving way a little to the thematic figure (+), the *sf* very pronounced, the opposing rhythms of the figure being clearly brought out (b):

Fig. 28

Ex. 2: Instead of pounding through the following passage (last movement of Haydn, Op. 76, No. 2) in a loud *forte* which makes it difficult to distinguish between *f* and *ff* and *fz* and causes the whole to sound monotonous and unintelligible, the introduction of a little variety quickly clarifies the situation. Something on this order: A vigorous but not strident *forte* to begin with. At the unison (a)—which, being very resonant, would sound too loud in proportion to what follows if all four continued in the same degree of *forte*—let each instrument play ever so little less *forte*, with the *fz*'s well marked. At (b) the last triplet of the unison passage may be slightly separated from what precedes and already a little broader, thus marking the entrance of the *ff*, to which it belongs. Through this *ff* the first violin plays out as loud as possible against the sustained chord of the lower voices. The first triplet of the next unison (c) is again separated as belonging to the following quarter-note, and, since there is shortly to be another *ff*, this unison may be taken only *forte*, the triplet (d) being treated as at (b), belonging to the *ff*. Noting that the first violin's Eb (at e) bears no *fz*, its second Eb and following D will give way to let the viola be heard with the theme in the original degree of *forte*. This now sweeps along, vigorously for the viola, singingly and not too loud for the violins (who are two against the one with the theme); is resumed once more by the first violin and carried to the change of key with perhaps a little greater breadth (but no ritard) as it approaches the final holds:

Allegro ma non troppo

Fig. 29

Ex. 3: Similar considerations apply in passages of a sustained *piano* or *pianissimo*. The subdued introduction to the first movement of Beethoven's Op. 74, with its *sotto*

voce opening, its sudden *forte* chord breaking into the calm —(no *crescendo* leads to it, though the two preceding measures are *espressivo!*)—calls for a special treatment of the last seven measures leading into the *Allegro*. The prolonged chromatic ascent of these bars tends to cause a rise in dynamic degree, but there should be none until the *crescendo* in the last bar. This tendency may be overcome if the first violin, after its thematic measure, restrains itself within a slightly softer *degree of piano* (the harmonic color of the phrase here takes on an almost mysterious quality) and then, to avoid sudden increase of tone where all four voices move (b), the whole remains at this level, the cello sounding through the others without playing any louder. Thus the suspense is sustained and the brief *crescendo* of the last bar enters dramatically into the *forte* tonic chord of the *Allegro*. (One may even *think pp* with a clear conscience to carry out the effect):

Fig. 30

II. In handling dynamic effects one must consider the *natural dynamic tendencies* of a phrase—just as in phrasing one considers the natural emphasis of the phrase-tones—and act in accord with them or counteract them, as the case may be.

Ex. 1: An ascending phrase, as we have just seen in Fig. 30, is apt to have a natural tendency to increase in tone with its building-up. Yielding to this tendency, unless so indicated by the composer, may produce a bad musical effect, a false dynamic expression. This would be the case in a phrase like the following (Beethoven, Op. 18, No. 1) in a quick *scherzo* movement and all in *piano*: the music is lighter and wittier if kept *piano*, and furthermore, this adds to the effectiveness of the indicated dynamics—*p, pp, ppp, cresc., sf, f, fp, ff*—that are to follow in the rest of the piece:

Fig. 31

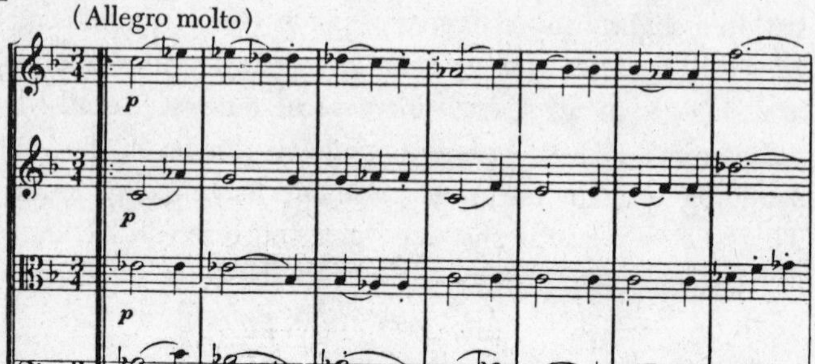

(Allegro molto)

Ex. 2: Again, by observing the exact part of the phrase in which an indicated *crescendo* or *diminuendo* takes place, one may avoid those involuntary alterations in volume of tone which may spoil the intended effect. A sensitive measure from the *Adagio* of the same Beethoven quartet is often misread in this respect by giving in to the tendency of the phrase to grow louder already on the last beat of the first

measure, whereas the *cresc.* is not meant to begin until the
next measure:

Fig. 32

If the two different treatments are played over and com-
pared, the original will readily be felt to be the finer.

Ex. 3: There are, however, instances where greater dynamic interest may be obtained by following the natural
inclination of the phrase, provided the delicacy of the music is not offended in intensifying the desired effect. The
following measures from the finale of the same Beethoven
(Op. 18, No. 1) as the music descends in semitones have a
tendency to diminish in volume, and by letting this inclination have play—perhaps during the repeated measures (a)
so that the two before the *cresc.* are the lowest dynamically, the bow dropping dryly on the string, without expression—the *cresc.* in its turn becomes more effective, big-
ger, before dropping back to *p*:

Fig. 33

III. Sometimes one needs to *make dynamic variations* where none are indicated. Here the natural tendencies of the phrase will be a useful guide in picking appropriate effects.

Ex. 1: A common habit we all take to in our earliest learning is that of playing a repeated phrase more softly the second time than the first, though there may be no indication to that effect. The difference may be very marked or very slight. Take this passage (from the first movement of Haydn's Op. 76, No. 1): since it is all in *piano* before the sudden return of the theme in *forte* some measures later, the repeated phrases beginning at measures 3 and 7 should obviously remain in grades of *piano*:

Fig. 34

Sometimes the effect may be reversed and, instead of echoing, the repeated measures may begin to build up towards a louder dynamic degree. The object is in either case to achieve dynamic variation that is appropriate to the style of the music.

Ex. 2: In Haydn or Mozart one frequently finds passages like the following (again Haydn, Op. 76. No. 1, first movement) which sound monotonous if played steadily through on one level. By playing them over several times thoughtfully, dynamic expressions suggest themselves. Certainly nothing extreme would be suitable since the composer would have indicated it if that had been his intention. Perhaps something of this sort: Beginning *forte*, one might, taking (a) as point of departure and without sacrificing the brilliance of the first violin's quality, after two or three measures very gradually indeed diminish during the cello's descending bass-line and against the held tones of the inner voices, to reach at (b)—where the eighth-note figure changes and the inner voices join in the activities, so that a fresh start is almost called for—a *mezzoforte* or even a not-too-soft *piano,* thence growing again through the faster dynamic rise to the big *ff*:

(Allegro con spirito)

Fig. 35

IV. Once the interpreters' minds are made up about the relative value of their *fortes* and *pianos* in a composition, they may find that the execution requires some *exaggeration*. Distinctions do not always carry to a distance—even the short distance of an individual just outside the group of four—but no matter how fine they may be there must be no doubt about them in the listener's ear. Reasons for this need of exaggeration will be more fully discussed in the following section.

The Pause or Lift

The pause is the great means of *clarifying and defining* to the listener. We have seen how valuable is the imperceptible wait in conveying phrases. The need now becomes apparent for a similar treatment in conveying sudden changes from one dynamic degree to another—*f* to *p*, *p* to *pp*, and their opposites—for in these sudden dynamic changes, as in phrasing, one sound-quality must finish before another enters.

The dynamic power of the pause is not a self-contradictory term. If the ear does not understand the progress of musical motion everything is muddled to it. Dynamic phrases—the pulse-lengths into which that motion is confined—should not succeed one another faster than the senses can apprehend them. It takes time for sound-waves to travel to the listener's ear, and, immeasurably microscopic as that time may be even in a concert hall, infinitesimal as it is in a room, it is nevertheless true that a sound-impression (as of a *forte* measure) remains dominant in the listener's brain for a longer instant than the player supposes. Its resonance covers the beginning and prevents the registration of any subsequently sent impression, particularly of a softer and less intense vibration, as of a *piano* following a *forte*. This is equally true of a softer impression (as of a *piano* measure) the resonance of which lingers a fraction of an instant beyond the beat which the player feels and which is rudely broken into if the succeeding impression (as of a *forte* or even of another *piano*) is too soon dispatched after it.

The human ear, moreover, is a very delicate mechanism which apprehends sound with many variations and subtleties and individual interpretations that are not written in the score from which the player broadcasts. When he has a particular effect in mind, therefore, he must articulate it so that there can be no doubt of his intention. To this end he may have to exaggerate to his own ear, to make, for the sake of distance, more of a pause between the end of a *forte* and the entrance of a *piano* than he would think necessary. Very soon his own ear will demand this pause, recognizing the greater clarity and plasticity it achieves.

He will appreciate its value most rapidly by listening to another group than his own, when he will be the first to look for clear enunciation. It will also help if he keeps always in mind the point of view of the listener.

I. Without a pause, most sudden dynamic contrasts simply remain unfulfilled. The extent of the pause can only be determined by the case.

Ex. 1: A triple *ppp* following a *ff* is not at all effective unless there is sufficient wait after the *ff* to let the entrance of the *ppp* be heard. The return of the *ff* after the *ppp* requires less of a pause because of the passing from a soft to a loud degree, but neither is it convincing without a tiny break, no more, really, than a fresh attack. The appropriate pauses are indicated by apostrophes in the following quotation from the *Scherzo* of the César Franck Quartet:

Fig. 36

Ex. 2: In a less extreme case, changing abruptly from *forte* to *piano*, a pause is still essential to make the inset of the *piano* clear (Beethoven, Op. 18, No. 1, first movement):

Fig. 37

Sometimes it is the accompaniment that makes the break before resuming its discourse in a softer degree, as in the same movement:

Fig. 38

Ex. 2a: In the same movement, again, will be found an example (Fig. 48) where, following a *ff*, the cello suddenly resumes the theme in *piano*. In such a case, the least lift will prevent everybody from falling hard on the already obvious C major resolution; and though second and viola (not quoted here) at this point are not marked *p* until their second eighth, they, together with the first violin, will drop down enough to allow the cello its chance to come through.

Ex. 3: Even the less drastic changes, as from *p* to *pp*, require a distinct pause to make the new statement tell fully, as here (again the same movement), there being no *diminuendo*, where the entrance of the relative key (A♭) brings a very effective harmonic change which Beethoven makes the most of by his dynamic marks:

Fig. 39

Ex. 4: Where a *forte* succeeds a *piano* without any preparatory *crescendo*, a tiny pause is also necessary, a pause that is no more, perhaps, than the imperceptible lift called for by the phrasing (from the last movement of the same quartet):

Fig. 40

and again (first movement of Op. 18, No. 2):

Fig. 41

II. Where there is *no change* in dynamic degree a pause may still be needed to *separate the resonance* of one phrase-group from that of the next.

Ex. 1: Such is the case in the following measures (first movement of Beethoven's Op. 18, No. 1) where even after the hold a slight break is necessary to register the inset of the second *ff*. A pause is of course needed before the *pp* because it introduces something new in a much softer dynamic degree. Note also that the hold remains *ff* throughout, and that the length of the E♭ and the C is indicated by the fact that Beethoven marks it not over the first but over the second measure, the first measure passing in tempo:

Fig. 42

III. Only the pause, furthermore, makes possible certain of the *finer effects* of dynamic variety.

Ex. 1: Chief of these, perhaps, is the device so characteristic of Beethoven—the *crescendo* leading, surprisingly, to a *piano*. This it is in no way possible to interpret save by a pause before the entrance of the *piano*. Compare the following example (from Op. 18, No. 1) with the related measures in Fig. 39. In this instance there is a normal modulation from a dominant seventh to its tonic (D♭–G♭), in *crescendo* and returning to the previous degree of *piano*, the resulting effect being quite different:

Fig. 43

Again, from the *Adagio affettuoso ed appassionato* of the same quartet:

Fig. 44

Fig. 32 provides another example from the same movement. Further characteristic cases will be found in the last movement of the same quartet as well as in any of the Op. 18's —in fact, it goes without saying, in any Beethoven Quartet.

Ex. 2: Where the *piano* is a *finish*, not introducing anything new as it does in the foregoing examples, the pause would be less, no more than the imperceptible wait or lift, so as not to interfere with the continuity of the phrase (again from the *Allegro con brio*. Op. 18, No. 1):

Fig. 45

Ex. 3: A tiny pause, again, is needed to convey a *piano subito* (Ravel, first movement, *Allegro moderato*):

Fig. 46

The above excerpt from Quartet by Ravel used by permission of A. Durand & Cie., Paris, France.

The Accent

The accent has many kinds of dynamic value. It runs through varying degrees, from the unwritten accent of the rhythmic pulse and rhythmic emphasis akin to the natural emphasis discussed under Phrasing, to the accent indicated by $>$ or *sf* or *fz*, by *fp* or the *mfp* and *sfp* one finds in Mozart scores. The accent may be slight, or heavy; it may be gentle, or rough (in which case, as we have seen, it is still not necessary to lift both feet off the floor to produce it). One would read an accent in Mozart differently from one in Bartók. Here again the style of the music first decides what degree of accentuation is necessary in proportion to what goes before and after. Then the acoustical problem of producing the accent so that it carries distinctly will suggest the best treatment.

I. It is a general experience of quartet players to find that the *sf* (*sforzato*) or *fz* (*forzando*) needs to be marked by a firmer or more brilliant attack than the individual player is at first disposed to give it. This is especially so in *forte* passages. To him the accent may sound decided enough, but a few paces away it is weak. While one may seek to avoid a persistent, tiresome harshness, it is easy to sound indifferent, and an indifferent accent is vague and ineffective. Whether strong or gentle, an accent must always be vital.

Ex. 1: A good, lively attack is wanted in all four voices in the following *forte* passage (first movement, Beethoven, Op. 127):

Fig. 47

Ex. 2: The same holds true for the following sustained notes which, being held in a good *forte*, will need to be separated to get a fresh bite on the string for each *sf* (first movement, Beethoven, Op. 18, No. 1):

Fig. 48

Here too it is important to bring out the *ff* of the three quarter-notes very vigorously, after which it is up to the cello to drop to the *p* theme with a complete change of character on his C (cf. p. 103, Ex. 2a).

Ex. 3: Beethoven's Op. 127 presents an opening difficult to produce with the needed power, conviction and clarity. The vigorous E♭ *sf* chord is repeated on the first, the rhythmically strongest beat of the second measure, but only as a dotted eighth, short and crisp. An imperceptible pause, a lift of the bow, must then emphasize the syncopation marked by the *sf* quarter-note, followed by another short, crisp eighth. The extension of this motive brings the *sf* back to the natural strong first beat of measure five (and, for the first violin, six) and these strong beats need also to be approached with a lift to give them the importance obviously theirs in the phrase. There is the double difficulty of keeping the tone heroic, large, full (the *Maestoso* really majestic) and yet playing the eighth-notes really short, very vibrant but not accented. This may be accomplished by a compact bow, as it were, drawing only so much on the long notes that the short ones have not too much return stroke to absorb:

Fig. 49

Ex. 4: A similar bite, with close bow, though in a faster tempo, helps to give the necessary character to the two down-bows at the opening statement of the theme in the Debussy Quartet.

Ex. 5: When the dynamic degree in which the *sf* occurs is *soft*, the accent is of course modified to a proper proportion. Sometimes it requires just a little more bow than the surrounding tones; sometimes it is achieved by no more than a quicker *vibrato*. In the *Andante scherzoso* theme of Beethoven's Op. 18, No. 4, the *sf* should not be harsh or abrupt but should stand out piquantly from the surrounding *pp*:

Fig. 50

Andante scherzoso, quasi allegretto

Had Beethoven written in later times he would probably have used the $>$ in such a place (he does use it in the first two announcements of the *Allegretto* theme in Op. 59, No. 1) rather than the more violent *sf*, but this mark is rare with him.

II.   The *fp* (*fortepiano*) is to be distinguished from the *sf* and *fz*. It may be produced not so much by a sharp inset as by a fuller volume of tone dropping instantaneously to a less full. It may be thought of as a larger, softer accent, but it too should be so distinctly made as to leave no doubt in the listener's ear.

The difference is well illustrated in the first movement of Beethoven's Quartet in F, Op. 18, No. 1. After the *stretto* passage (quoted in Fig. 28) a drop to *piano* is made through holding the *forte* quality for an instant and letting it fall almost at once to *piano*. The inner voices play an important role here, for after the slight prolongation of the first eighth to convey the needed emphasis they are responsible for re-establishing the tempo in the changed dynamic:

(Allegro con brio)

Fig. 51

As the passage proceeds, each entrance is made with this fuller tone dropping at once to *piano*, in contradistinction to the much earlier appearance of the figure in *piano* with sharp *sf* inset, thus:

Fig. 52

Other *fp* marks in the same movement may be similarly distinguished from the *sf*:

Fig. 53

III. One finds in Mozart not only *fp* and *sf*, *mfp* and *sfp* (though not yet the $>$) but a variety of characteristic dynamic indications. For example: in the G Major Quartet (K. 387) the alternating *p* and *f* of the *Menuetto's* theme:

p f p. -f p f etc.;

in the first movement of the Bb (K. 589) this:

mf p . mf p | mf p | mf f | f

and in the Trio of its *Menuetto* this:

p sfp | p ‖

indicating that the half-note is held loud, the drop to *p* being on the first beat of the next measure; and in the A

Major (K. 464) the *Menuetto* theme again: All these want thinking about in order to be effectively presented. The Trio of the last-mentioned piece provides a particularly interesting study in dynamic variety.

IV. There is another type of accent that is *tenuto* rather than attacked.

Ex. 1: Since the following passage is in *piano*, the *fz* occurring in it will be full rather than sharp, so that here the violin may mark its E♯ rather by a little more *vibrato* and a least lingering—in agreement with the cello, of course, as they move to the 6/4 of the coming B minor, this expansion being made up for by at once picking up tempo in the sixteenths (first movement of Haydn's Op. 76, No. 5):

(Allegretto)

Fig. 54

Ex. 2: Considering the romantic spirit of Brahms's *Allegretto* movements, and also the indication *semplice* (simply), the theme of the third movement of the C Minor Quartet is yet often painfully misconceived by quartet players because they fail to take into account its peculiar sensitiveness to the false accentuation that attends any unevenness of tone production. The second sixteenth in each group of two, unless carefully evened, naturally tends to be weaker than the first, and this in turn causes the first to sound as though it bore an intentional accent in addition to that of its rhythmic position. Add to this the steady drumming of the dotted eighths in second violin and cello and you find this tendency to sound accented on every beat of the measure. But evidently Brahms intended only the fourth beat to be marked, giving the lilt that characterizes the phrase. Something must be done to counteract the choppy effect of an accent on each beat. If the lower voices moderate their tone as finely as possible, only the viola's figure standing out, the first violin keeps its sixteenths even and smooth, and if all four together feel this fourth beat with a slight lift or *tenuto* (*vibrato* plus a little more bow), it will be thrown easily, not roughly accented, to the fore:

Fig. 55

V. Control of the rhythmic accent is of great importance dynamically, as well as in phrasing, because of the tone-volume inherent in accent which may need to be set free or suppressed.

Ex. 1: A chord passage needs watching in this respect because a harmonic progression may tend to accumulate strength as it advances. In a phrase that is heading toward a high-point or a resolution this effect can be given free play, as at the close of a section or movement (Haydn, Op. 76, No. 1, first movement):

(Allegro con spirito)

Fig. 56

But in the *introductory* measures of the same movement, where the chords simply break ground for the theme to enter, it is better to start right out with full tone, a bold beginning, with emphasis on the first chord; then to avoid increasing the tone as the range of the chord expands, for such increase would tend to broaden the tempo and delay the inset of the chords, thus destroying the sense of leading up to the theme, of setting the stage for what is to come, which is the purpose of the introduction. One must overcome one's timidity at striking a chord into the blue without notice; also the natural tendency of the high third, the B of the first violin, to ring out disproportionately loud:

(Allegro con spirito)

Fig. 57

Ex. 2: A sure rhythmic accent is needed in the *forte* motif that occurs in the two 3-measure groups at bars 27-32 (contrasting with the 4-measure rhythm of the theme and in some editions marked *Ritmo di tre battute*) in the *Scherzo* of Beethoven's Op. 127. For the violin's highest note, G, and also the chord progression, tend to emphasize the last of the three quarter-notes whereas it is the *first* quarter which gives the three-measure rhythm its character:

Fig. 58

(Scherzando vivace)

VI. Like the imperceptible wait or lift which proves so useful in phrasing, there is also what might be called the *imperceptible accent.* It is that slight accentuation which makes clear the entrance of a note and it may be used to follow such a wait.

We have already seen how, as a phrase, the following measures are not significant unless the repeated chord keeps persistently alive and fresh, and this is difficult to achieve in face of the monotony bred of the very repetition unless the long tied note is *finished* and, after the imperceptible wait, the renewed tone (a) sets in with an imperceptible accent. This handling provides an easy escape from the tendency to *push* the tied quarter, an unimportant note falling, or in this case lying over, on an accented beat. Then comes the imperceptible wait to point the change from *f* to *p*, while in the next measure an imperceptible accent is wanted in the viola's modulating voice (b) which provides the next change-tone in harmony, color and dynamic. (Haydn, Op. 76, No. 1):

(Allegro con spirito)

Fig. 59

VII. The type of accent which is really no more than *marked rhythmic accuracy* may be of great service in clarifying a complex passage where correct phrasing alone is not enough.

Ex. 1: This development passage (last movement, Mozart, D, K. 499), in which two rather inarticulately brief thematic fragments—one in triplets, the other in eighths and sixteenths—are fighting for supremacy, may result in a muddled effect. But the confusion is at once cleared away if each instrument takes care that every one of its own notes sounds out equally, that the sixteenths especially be not neglected in their brevity, and that the triplets be well-rounded and emphatic:

(Allegro)

Fig. 60

Ex. 2: This sort of definite rhythmic accent preserves the value of short quick notes and thereby also the accuracy of phrasing which may otherwise be disturbed. How frequently one hears the *Scherzo* of Beethoven's Op. 74 (the "Harp") played as though it opened with a triplet ♪♪♩ instead of three eighths ♪♪♩!:

Fig. 61

The rhythmic test of these notes is in their fitting with the steady eighths of the second violin and viola, which in turn must not yield to the tendency of sounding like a 6/8 rhythm with two accents. This test becomes especially neat later on where the violins move in octave sequences, the second starting its four eighths on the second beat of the measure while the lower voices provide the two eighths on the first beat:

Fig. 62

The three notes may be evened by thinking of the dotted quarter, which bears the main rhythmic accent and at which they aim, and remembering the natural third-beat accent on the second eighth, the three making a long up-beat. Not too much bow on the dotted quarter, so that one comes back easily on the three eighths, as indeed the "*f leg-giermente*" suggests, and the problem is solved.

To preserve the same proper rhythm in the unison after the double bar these three notes may be bowed thus, back and forth in the lower quarter of the bow:

Fig. 63

(This bowing may be useful at other moments as well, and in other sections of the bow, to give the dotted quarter its full value and yet prevent any gasping effect of getting back into position for the three eighths.)

The accuracy of rhythmic emphasis under discussion is particularly important in this movement. For upon arriving at the *Più presto quasi prestissimo* the rhythm suddenly does turn over into a 6/8. So that there should be no doubt of this, Beethoven marks the section "*Si ha s'imaginar la battuta di* 6/8—to be imagined in a beat of 6/8." The tempo in both cases is so fast that one counts only *one* to a meas-ure; i.e., two bars of the three quarter-notes in the *Più presto* are equivalent to one in the *Presto* (which, though it contains six eighths, is not "in 6/8"!). Therefore one need not be surprised to see the same metronome mark over each, namely, $\downarrow. = 100$.

SEVEN

Color and Texture

COLOR AND TEXTURE are, of course, the elements that give quartet music its special character, that typify this particular crystallization of musical thought. The texture produced by the four homogeneous instruments provides a variety, both extensive in range and highly refined, of those differentiations in tonal quality which, together with harmonic values and dynamics, make for what we call color. Once the quartet player puts his mind on the possibilities involved, he will find himself in a field of thought and work that is fascinating, challenging, exacting of his best.

He is now faced with the problem: How to interpret indications of color? How to carry out the textural interest and significance the composer may have had in mind? He has almost no guides. How to read from the music where there are no specific indications? Dynamic marks, *pianos* and *fortes*, dots, dashes, slurs; sometimes words: *dolce, marcato, cantabile, espressivo, agitato, lusingando, teneramente,* Beethoven's famous *beklemmt* (as if oppressed, anxious) in the Cavatina of the big B♭, Op. 130. But for the most part nothing—only the music itself. Ravel, in his lively second movement, says *"quasi arpa*—like a harp" to distinguish a variation of the *pizzicato* theme, but Beethoven, in the first movement of Op. 74, says nothing at all over the *pizzicato* arpeggios which are its characteristic figure and which have caused the Quartet to be popularly known as the "Harp" Quartet.

Color, moreover, like dynamics, is relative. A dotted note may have to sound rather longer or shorter in one type of phrase or movement than in another; a *piano* or a *forte* rather fuller or thinner because of what precedes or follows it; a contrast vivid or only mild. Sometimes *thinking* an effect is enough, where it is too subtle for any written indication. Usually, however, the execution requires some exaggeration to convey the thought. There is still always the problem of achieving acoustically the composer's and the player's intentions, and the same considerations of distance and the listener apply here as in the treatment of dynamics.

The quartet player must cultivate his feeling for texture, his color ear. If the student realizes this from the first, he will constantly listen for color values, listen to himself and to his colleagues not only for the sake of the ensemble but indeed for the very life and interest of his performance. For music may be afflicted with a peculiar dullness which deadens even the most beautiful phrases if the presentation is not kept vivid and purposeful. The clear purity of the four-voice texture particularly needs to be kept clean, sparkling, fluent, like the pure waters of a stream that come to a dull stagnation if they do not flow.

Color interest has grown in the development of music until the modern ear undoubtedly demands much of it. Early quartet manuscripts, as we have seen, bore almost no marks; the texture was too simple, the musical thought itself too limited, it seems to us now, to make any great call on range of expression. But the technique of both composer and player grew as their means became more complex. We probably endow Haydn and Mozart with more variety of textural color than they received from the players of their own time, to judge by the history of technique. We have unconsciously and inevitably applied our own methods, and as we have seen, it is no sin to keep their musical thought alive by our own warmth and by the variety of color we in our more complex state find necessary, provided we remain within the bounds of their style. We consult tradition, avoid the grotesque, try to exercise good taste, bearing in mind always the sense and style of the music. These, then, for lack of more exact indications, must be the quartet player's guides in determining what use to make of his technical resources.

That he will probably tax them all becomes apparent the moment he analyzes his problem. He has not only to determine the relative values of his dynamic effects. He must consider the *quality of tone* of the different instruments; the fact that a prominent voice moving against a background of *its own texture* may need some distinction of treatment; the effect of a modulation or the definite establishment of a key; the quality of sound produced by a unison of two or more voices, and also of the separate strings played upon; the emphasis inherent in a tone or group of tones in their melodic or harmonic significance. The bow needs quite special study as a giver of color: its effect near the bridge or near the fingerboard, the length and type of stroke needed, the importance and variety of its uses in accompaniment-figures, the quality of *spiccato* or *legato* required in a particular passage, and so forth.*

For purposes of practice a little realistic suggestion may be valuable. It is a human habit to form pictures in the mind. Our very ideals are of this nature. Pictures may be helpful and they are legitimate so long as they are not permitted to substitute themselves for the original intention of another man's mind. We are at liberty to imagine the

---

* The achieving of the more purely mechanical bowed-instrument effects like the *tremolo* and the *ponticello* comes down to well-controlled technical accomplishment and need hardly be illustrated here. More extreme stunts, like slapping the strings with the stick, or producing the peeps, squeaks and groans of Webernesque compositions, also have their place but are not discussed here since they may safely be left to the imagination, skill and hardihood of the performers.

vigorous galloping of a knight on horseback if it helps us to an ensemble feeling of Haydn's opening phrase (Op. 74, No. 3):

(Allegro)

Fig. 64

But we must not then assume that Haydn wanted to convey any such idea when his was a purely musical inspiration: it was not the composer but the popular inclination to form a picture-in-the-mind that christened this the "Ritter (Cavalier) Quartet". The use of such realistic suggestion is to help crystallize your own idea and make it clear to others; it is a tool for achieving an effect, not for persuading the listener to take over anything but the intended vigorous *musical* effect. *Think* brilliance if it will give life to a brilliant passage; *think* sweetness, smooth singing of a human voice, if it will give life to a *cantabile*; *think* tragedy and sorrow, *think* joy, humor, merriment, *think* any picture of these human moods and manifestations if it will make the color of the music more vital to your mind and enable you so to render it.

To give his students a picture of the sort of close, chatty *spiccato* that would carry out the effect of the following measures from the last movement of Haydn's Quartet in C (Op. 74, No. 1), an experienced quartet player described them as being like "little women huddled together gossiping in the marketplace":

Fig. 65

Such a picture may certainly be said to be borne out by the music itself, which here restates the theme through a variation in which the voices come closer together than before, in criss-crossing bits of contrary motion, briefly peck out a different chord on each eighth, all equally busy with the tight, choppy sort of bowing called for by the indication *staccato assai*.

Sometimes it is a *sense* one is aware of rather than a concrete picture. Of noble exaltation, as in the *Adagio* of Beethoven's Op. 127 (Fig. 27); of the remote and ethereal, as in the coda of the same movement (Fig. 72); of hollowness, as in the *Largo* of Haydn's Op. 76, No. 5 (because of the harmonic progressions, Fig. 119, measures 5-7); of wistfulness, as in the *Allegretto* of the Brahms C minor (Fig. 55); and so on, at the pleasure of the individual. Many thoughts of this kind one keeps to oneself. They may turn out to be sentimental imaginings. The pictures of a more practical nature one may lay before one's colleagues if there is question of trying for some particular effect.

Ravel's *"quasi arpa"* for certain chords of harp-like effect may be called a suggestion from the composer for a picture in the player's mind to be conveyed by him to the listener. But such indications are rare, and for the most part the player has to evolve his own pictures. Sometimes, however, a composer all unwittingly offers some realistic suggestion in the strength of his own preoccupation, as carried in his style, his idiom. Take César Franck. With his dynamic range from finespun *ppp* to grand *ff*, his long, unbroken lines, the fullness of his inner voices, the sweep and swell of his accompaniment figures, his frequent *largamente* and *sostenuto*—as in the *Larghetto* of the Quartet—by all this the texture and color of his music reveal the organist's feeling for sustained expression. Naturally the aim of the players will be to re-create this feeling, whether or not they need to daydream images of the organ-loft of Sainte Clotilde.

National elements in music also suggest a kind of realism, intangible though they may be. Some music is interesting chiefly because of its national traits, because its themes and color reproduce the folk music and the life-spirit of a country. These traits therefore must be preserved. Other music is built upon folk material either deliberately or because it lies deeply embedded in the composer's own conceptions (one thinks of Kodály, and of many of our own composers), so that its execution calls for every musical consideration besides that of its national color which it must be given if it is to remain characteristic. A Hungarian player will give the dash, rhythm and color of his native music with no special thought, because it is in his blood, but an Anglo-Saxon or a Latin player may have to make conscious efforts to master these characteristics. He may take suggestions from hearing a native interpreter, or he may be helped through the functioning of an artistic imagination by a picture-in-his-mind—of the plains of Hungary, vast, lost in a haunting solitude, to guess from the slow movement of Kodály's first quartet—of the peasant scenes and dances, the national-life color with which the music is tinged. Then there is the subtler sort of national trait such as one finds here and there in a phrase or rhythmic or melodic figure of Brahms: the graceful languor of Viennese elegance, the swing and vigor of the waltz, the folk-song quality of so many of his themes. The color-values of such elements may be largely understood through a wide knowledge of the composer's works and taken up in the performing quartet's own style.

If in the following attempt to show how quartet material may be analyzed in the service of color and texture the music may seem to be sacrificed to theories of execution and forcibly broken into unrelated fragments, this is only for purposes of study. In arranging what might be termed the *color-scheme* of any movement or series of movements, the music *as a whole* must always be borne in mind. In the "classics," for example, it would be poor style to employ several different color-values * in the first measures of a movement—in fact, the music itself would make this impossible—and better to reserve contrasts and new effects for the developmental sections; the more distant repetitions

---

* An exception at once comes to mind in the Mozart *Menuetto* discussed under Dynamics (p. 112) where such values spring from the dynamic indications in the score!

and more complex reproductions may need different or more emphatic treatment than those first heard. In later, colorful, romantic music, on the other hand, it may be necessary to employ many different qualities of color in the very first announcements of the thematic material. In short, the color and textural values must be apportioned according, once more as always, to the style and the sense of the music.

Types of Short and Long Notes *

I. A note with a dot above it is supposed to be short. But the player's problem only begins here. How short? What kind of brevity: dry, or resonant? Chopped off, or slightly *tenuto*? There are two kinds of dots used in earlier scores of Haydn and Mozart, one the long dot ▾, the other an ordinary dot • ; the former as a rule is interpreted as sharp, the latter as short or simply meaning separation.

Ex. 1: The first movement of Haydn's G Minor Quartet (Op. 74, No. 3) shows how in a short space the selfsame marks may be variously interpreted. First, eight bars of vigorous dotted quarters, grace notes very clear but not long, played in the lower third of the bow to give strength to the galloping rhythm, even the final quarter short, since it automatically carries a shade more emphasis because of its position (Fig. 64). Then two measures rest, a pause before something new is to happen. Now the cello re-establishes the chord, but *piano*, with light notes not themati-

---

* No attempt has been made here to look into original editions of the music discussed. Most of us are dependent on some sort of editorial help, and for our general purposes recognized editions have seemed adequate. To go deeper into the matter would require special study. It would probably also turn up some alternative suggestions.

cally announced but softly introductory to what we are
about to hear:

Fig. 66

This the viola starts with its two quarter-notes, again
dotted. But should these two dotted quarters sound like
either of the two types just heard? Observe the slur over
the dots which may indicate something more than that
the notes are to be taken in the same bow. This is a new
theme, gentle, slightly plaintive, and should enter *as
something new*, both for its own musical value and to convince the listener. Try a slightly sticky bow, slightly *tenuto*
in spirit without delaying the tempo, as though the notes
had been marked ⌣. At once a new color is achieved.
There is the needed musical distinction.

This figure is repeated through varying dynamic degrees
and should never lose its characteristic quality. Then, in
the fifty-fourth measure, it happens again. Still it is not to
be assumed that the two quarters are to be played in just
the same way. Here they are evidently introductory to the
theme that begins *piano* in the next measure. The violin is
alone and can do more or less what it pleases with them.
They are, thus, a bond between the preceding and the
subsequent matter. They also progress from loud to soft.
Let them, therefore, be thought of as bearing a diminishing dynamic (a), sounding perfectly free, held back a little

affectedly so that the tempo may be resumed promptly
on the new theme. The dotted quarters in this light and
joking melody can be really short and merry, while the
figure (b) sounds full and singing in contrast:

Fig. 67

This theme is repeated with a secondary triplet figure
which finally spins itself into:

Fig. 68

The three final eighths should be very short indeed, delicate and sprightly to distinguish them even from the merry
quarters that preceded—all three upbow, as the change to
a down-stroke would be too heavy.

Ex. 2: Staccato quarters, again, may require the *piquancy*
of consecutive upbows (like the eighths just mentioned),

as in the first movement, *Allegro con spirito*, of Haydn's G
Major Quartet, Op. 76, No. 1:

Fig. 69

(Allegro con spirito)

Ex. 3: Another type of dotted note, the *broad staccato*,
is the good shooting *martelé*, in middle and upper bow,
long enough to avoid being dry and literal (as a Kreutzer
study taken nearer the point would sound), but crisp
enough to avoid getting sloppy and uncharacteristic. The
example quoted (from the *Allegretto con variazioni* of
Beethoven's Op. 74) is sometimes played with a heavy
staccato near the frog. The first method is perhaps the one
with more swing:

Fig. 70

(Allegretto)

Ex. 4: A *softer staccato*, like a subdued *martelé*, is useful
in passages that are not merely accompaniment but have

a secondary thematic importance, as in the cello and first violin parts of the following example. This is made in the upper third of the bow, the entrance of each note piquant, but the bow allowed to shoot, not actually lifted, the length to the next stroke, so that the tone rings on consecutively and is yet clear-cut on each note (from the *Adagio molto espressivo* section of the great *Adagio* in Beethoven's Op. 127):

Fig. 71

This bowing holds good through *piano* and a firm *crescendo* (and in *forte* perhaps bringing the bow back nearer the bridge) and it appears again in the remote, ethereal *pp* of the coda, where it is used gently and near the fingerboard:

Fig. 72

For bowings of the inner voices through these passages see Exs. 10-11, p. 148ff., Figs. 98-101.

Ex. 5: When several dotted notes are included under a slur they may be meant to be not short, but simply separated (Mozart, D Minor, K. 421; see also Ex. 7, below):

Fig. 73

Ex. 6: Or a dot over the last note under a slur may simply mean that the note is *dropped*, not held literally, nor separated from the preceding note, but eased off. In the first illustration (Beethoven, Op. 18, No. 1), all the parts being alike marked with a dot, the viola, if it changes bow on its repeated notes, must watch that they are not heavier than the final notes in the other voices. In the second (Op. 74, theme of the last movement), only the first violin has the dot, and the accompanying voices, being slurred over, should watch that their final eighths are not held too long or let resound too heavily under the short eighth of the solo voice:

Fig. 74

Fig. 75

Ex. 7: Sometimes the resonance of a dotted note has, on the contrary, to be *lengthened* to carry over a rest, though it should not fill that rest by being held. This is done by means of a swift stroke, drawn as though for a much longer stroke than is actually taken (see also II, Ex. 3, below). In the following illustrations this swift stroke is followed by a swift catching-back of the bow to the point at which the next eighth is produced: in the first case (Mozart, D Minor, K. 421) the two eighths with rest between are full-length and smooth, being in a singing *andante*; in the faster *allegretto* (Mozart, F Major, K. 590) felt in two beats, they are short and light, with only a little and swifter bow:

Fig. 76

Fig. 77

II.   Unmarked notes, ordinary-looking eighths or quarters, may, because of their value in the phrase or theme and their color interest, need some distinguishing treatment.

Ex. 1: Beethoven writes *teneramente* (tenderly) over the opening of the *allegro* theme in Op. 127. Without this indication the quarter-notes could easily be played in a dull, almost mechanical progression. The effect may be achieved, perhaps, by a *feeling of quality* too delicate for any conventional mark, a least sensitive dwelling (but without delaying) upon each note, the last Ab, however, dotted under the slur, shortened by an easing of the bow, not quite a lift:

Fig. 78

Ex. 2: The two eighth-notes in the theme of the "Harp" Quartet (Beethoven, Op. 74) should never be slighted or they will lack character:

Fig. 79

The figure in which they occur is used throughout the movement in many different ways, observation of which suggests the best way of handling them. They appear *legato* in the dialogue of the violins, and next as a building-fragment in which, instead of being slurred, they are separated:

Fig. 80

Now the weak beats of the measure are accented, in *fortissimo*, and the first of the eighths bears a *sf*:

Fig. 81

Now again they play an important cohesive role in the weaving of the sequences through the three upper voices:

Fig. 82

In all these cases they are significant. Upon their first appearance their being on a weak beat should not lead to their sounding casual or trivial; they should be round and full. The quality needed is too subtle to be marked by even as much as an infinitesimal *tenuto*; but let it be *thought* and the playing kept close and smooth. When separated, again, they should not be neglected; rather, they have almost a slightly sticky quality.

Ex. 3: We have seen (Phrasing, I, Ex. 4) that sometimes a note should be dropped rather than held its written length. The contrary is also true. The quarter-notes in Fig. 8 would be dull and dead if they were to *sound* only for exactly their written length. At the same time they should not be dragged out. The dilemma may be solved by producing tones that will ring *after the bow leaves the string*. Here, in diminishing dynamic, is needed the swiftly drawn bow that is *on* the string only for the time indicated by the note, but, by being drawn fast and removed from the string while still in forward motion, causes the tone to continue sounding. This resonance—which is also helped if the finger does not quit the string but continues its *vibrato*—naturally does not cover the entire duration of the rests, but it leaves a sense of something more to come which prevents those rests from seeming like holes to the player's eye or the listener's ear.

Ex. 4: This resonant sort of tone is useful in accompanying or secondary supporting tones like those of the lower voices in the following measures from the *Adagio* of Beethoven's Op. 18, No. 1:

Fig. 83

Note also that the first violin's sixteenth-notes, moving against the background of this support and embroidering its harmonies with passing-notes, will require a flowing but plastic quality, with a close bow, expressive but simple.

The Spiccato

The *spiccato* bow presents a very particular problem in string quartet technic. The rapid springing notes that sound so clear, piquant and brilliant from the bow of a single violinist do not always carry so well where three or four voices join, but are liable to produce a chopping effect, lacking in resonance, insusceptible to blending, and unsatisfactory to the ear.

This may in part be due to the fact that quartet music calls for as subdued a technique as possible and the choppy brilliance of the *spiccato* many soloists use makes each instrument too conspicuous. In fact, ensemble playing calls for several varieties of *spiccato*. One has only to bear in mind its possible gradations "from snow and rain to hail."

I. If there is no reason for a *spiccato* figure or passage to stand out suddenly from the surrounding texture, one would naturally choose one of the gentler gradations.

Ex. 1: The first violin's sixteenths in Fig. 37, for example, would be smooth and quiet.

Ex. 2: Where fragmentary figures are passed from one voice to another, a smooth *carrying* quality is desirable: (Beethoven, Op. 59, No. 1, first movement):

 Fig. 84

The quality must remain the same through the four voices, and the enchainment will be made easier if a *flattish spiccato* is used. The two lower voices, being in unison at the octave, should watch that their figure is not too heavy, still *piano* before the *fp*.

Note that the whole passage from which Fig. 84 is taken, like similar passages, both *spiccato* and *legato,* throughout this first movement of Op. 59, No. 1, shows the importance of being *forehanded* by keeping the bow near the string (cf. comment to Figs. 1 and 9). For it is only by this readiness to *pick up* and to *hand over* the fragment that the voices will enchain properly. In the current of the ensemble (see p. 23) each player should feel that he is playing the whole passage, otherwise he risks beginning late and ending abruptly by dropping his phrase as though it were not connected with the next player's, as though it were finished with his share of it. Other examples of the importance of this ensemble sense will be found in Figs. 115 and 126 and in such passages as measures 12-14 of the first movement of the Mozart D Minor.

II. Then again any one of the four instruments having a solo passage of *spiccato* may have to stand out against a background of more sustained texture, and its tones should not be too brief or they count for nothing.

Ex. 1: A hard *spiccato* would be both awkward and tiresome in the *Vivace* of Haydn's Quartet in D (Op. 64, No. 5) and the character of the movement (not a *prestissimo*, as one sometimes hears it performed) calls for a closer, lightly bouncing sort of *sautillé* (unless the fiddler is blest with an exceptionally *fine spiccato*):

Fig. 85

Ex. 2: All through the first violin's extended passage against the sustained progressions of the other instruments (Beethoven, Op. 59, No. 1) the ear demands notes long enough to impress the meaning of the passing tones as a short *spiccato* could not do:

Fig. 86

Ex. 3: Clear articulation of the cello and viola duet in the *Canzonetta* of Mendelssohn's Op. 12 is extremely difficult because the thick low strings scarcely vibrate to a minute bow, yet the *pp* forbids too heavy a stroke. A quick flat *spiccato* will sound clearer than a bouncing one (the same being true for the violins, although their duet lies easier and a more brilliant stroke would be in place):

Fig. 87

III. Where the whole harmonic texture of a passage is being conveyed in *spiccato* each of the rapidly passing tones needs its full value in order that the ear may be convinced beyond a doubt of the intended progressions. What does the music demand? A comparison of two superficially somewhat similar *scherzo* movements of Beethoven—the *Andante scherzoso quasi Allegretto* from Op. 18, No. 4 and the *Allegretto vivace e sempre scherzando* from Op. 59, No. 1—will illustrate a certain fine distinction in the use of the bow. The quieter character of the *Andante* makes possible the production of more piquant tones than are feasible in the *Allegretto*, though in louder places the stroke will naturally flatten and lengthen to produce enough sound. The harmonic writing in the *Andante*, moreover, is far simpler, containing fewer progressions, octaves and repeated tones:

Fig. 88

than that in the *Allegretto*, where the voices move more independently and change harmonies constantly:

Fig. 89

Only a subdued *spiccato*, very even throughout the quartet, giving resonance to each note, will enable the ear to grasp the complex progressions of the second example; a skipping bow leaves them dry and soundless.

IV. Considerations such as these were perhaps what Brahms had in mind when he remarked that the virtuoso's *spiccato* rarely has place in the performance of quartet music. His own music certainly demands fullness in every passage, long resonance from notes that look short on paper, to bring out the richness of his thought in color and quality. The first movement of the C Minor Quartet is thoroughly characteristic: the long, flat *spiccato* accompaniment to the opening theme (a); the varied phases of the figure (b) in lighter *spiccato*, nearer middle of bow when in *piano* (and note the second violin's quarters dotted under the slur to give a resonant brevity); the heavy *forte* notes, long *spiccato* (*détaché*) near the frog (c):

Fig. 90

V. Further uses of *spiccato* as they occur in characteristic accompaniment figures will be referred to in the following section under detached notes.

Varieties of Accompaniment

The steady figure, usually in eighths or sixteenths, the downright accompaniment that serves principally to give harmonic background, is one of the most general means of producing color and textural effects. It is not enough to read notes slurred or separated, *forte* or *piano*. They may be written exactly alike in very different types of music; or in one spot they may be called upon to convey one color, in another, something else.

I. *Detached notes* provide a great variety of background color.

Ex. 1: At the opening of Beethoven's Op. 59, No. 1 (Fig. 22), second violin and viola provide an accompaniment in steady undotted eighths which if played in an ordinary *spiccato* does not satisfy the ear. Only a subdued longish stroke, whereby the eighths are just perceptibly detached, becomes the serenity of the cello's theme. Tone there must be, but in getting the right resonance the two voices need to guard against sounding too loud. It is their role to maintain a background for the melody, establishing the rhythm by slightly marking the two eighths of the naturally emphatic first beat—to help start the cello off, as it were—and dropping at once to their steady task, governed, of course, by the pulse of the solo part.

Ex. 2: In the opening of the Haydn D Minor (Op. 76, No. 2) the second violin, viola and cello play a vigorous, broadly detached stroke, not abrupt but vibrant, almost as though written: ♩♩♩ to set the minor key and support the first violin's sonorous theme in fifths. This means using the lower quarter of the bow, near the frog:

Fig. 91

The same figure opens the second half of the movement, but with the parts reversed, the upper voices heavy to meet the cello's solo. Later it appears in *piano*, again not as a skipping *spiccato* but as a vibrant *détaché*, with less bow, taken a little higher up, to give softer color and gentler texture.

Ex. 3: The second half of the opening phrase of Mozart's D Minor (K. 421) apparently offers a parallel, but here each three dotted eighths are under a slur, i.e., in one bow. The effect of this bowing in *forte* is quite different from the Haydn example preceding, requiring both a smoother and more clinging bow, all hairs on the string, bow scarcely lifted, but marking the detachment of each note with a little biting start, moving from upper middle to near frog and back:

Fig. 92

The four bars which open the movement *sotto voce*, and which are a first statement of the *forte* phrase, would call for a similar stroke with, of course, less bow, upper middle, perhaps a little towards the fingerboard for color, to furnish an appropriate background for the softness of the melody.

Ex. 4: The jovial opening of Haydn's G Major (Op. 54, No. 1) needs a brisker bowing than that in Ex. 2, but still a little broader and flatter than *spiccato*, obtained by using the lower portion of the bow:

Fig. 93

When the viola drops to *piano* it keeps a similar stroke, in a less dynamic degree, fresh and vibrant, while the cello and first violin treat the chromatic dotted eighths as *slightly* detached only, in one long upbow, since they are *thematic* and should stand out against the *accompanying* eighths of the viola.

Ex. 5: A more clinging, singing, smooth bow, on the other hand, only just noticeably detached (middle and upper middle) is required of the accompanying voices in the *Allegretto* of the same quartet to fit the singing quality of the violin's melody:

Fig. 94

The dotted eighths in the following *forte* measures, again, could not, owing to the style of the piece in general and because they represent the biggest moment in the whole movement (the 6/4 chord heading for the central cadence in the dominant) be a brittle or pointed *staccato* but should be full in tone, a broad *détaché* just above the frog:

Fig. 95

Ex. 6: The dotted quarters in the *Largo* of Haydn's Op. 76, No. 5 call for a sustained quality; they would obviously lose dignity if played *staccato* or sharply separated after the broad, organlike effect of the opening *cantabile e mesto* theme. But they must not drag, these three voices underlying the violin's figure. The best effect is obtained, perhaps, if the bow is drawn smoothly along and each quarter marked as with an accent, a little push to the bow, which will give the effect of a pulse, renewing but not breaking the wave-length of the tone. This avoids any tendency to stick and preserves the movement forward as a slowly pulsating current into which the violin's figure rhythmically fits:

(Largo)

Fig. 96

Ex. 7: Dotted eighths like those in Fig. 73 (from the *Andante* of the Mozart D minor, K. 421), on the contrary, do require a rather sticky bow. As each group repeats the same chord, unaltered except in the important second violin progressions at (a), it is well to maintain their quality, distinctly separated but closely adhesive to the string.

Ex. 8: In the Haydn *Largo* just cited (Ex. 6; see also Ex. 1, p. 167) there are in the interlude before the return to the beginning, ten measures of steady accompanying eighth-notes:

Fig. 97

The detachment here should be veiled, fitting in with the viola's (and subsequently the cello's) *piano* tone-quality, passing off with a certain flat colorlessness (upper portion of bow) which is very effective in the unusual harmonic changes. But as the tone-volume increases in the *crescendo* measure it should take on more color, fullness and vibrancy, the eighths should be adhesively lengthened until in the concluding *forte* they give again (separated, lower portion of bow) the organlike effect which characterizes the opening of the piece. The markings indicated offer a suggestion for their treatment.

Ex. 9: The last movement of the same quartet (Fig. 1) presents yet another value of the dot. Here the whole material is built on a lively figure in which the dotted notes are really short (a) and in *forte* need a direct chopping action of the bow, at frog, all hairs on string (b). When the viola and second violin, therefore, start their accompanying figure in *piano* (c) it must be with a crisp and unflagging precision (like saying ta ta-ta-ta ta ta-ta-ta) in a very close *spiccato*, well controlled, in which each note must sound equal, instantaneous, with mechanical persistence.

Ex. 10: The accompaniment figure running through the *Tempo I.* passage of the *Adagio* from Beethoven's Op. 127 goes through many stages of dynamic value and so of color value, from its *pianissimo* entrance:

(Adagio molto esp.)

Tempo I (Adagio)

Fig. 98

through the various *pianos* and *crescendos*, and through the measures quoted in Fig. 71, to the growing, constantly renewed *rinforzando* that eventually builds up a large body of tone:

Fig. 99

Perhaps a vibratoless *pianissimo* to mark the change of key, E—E♭, at (a) in Fig. 98; then very *quiet* detached groups of three (upper portion of bow) at (b), more bow naturally being used for the *crescendo* in Fig. 99; and finally in the *rinforzando* (c) separate and very vibrant strokes (lower portion of bow).

Ex. 11: In the coda of the same movement occurs that remote, ethereal passage (Fig. 72) which only the bow on the fingerboard, drawn with a soft, windy quality, can produce (a), coming back to the usual position on the strings again with the *crescendo* into the fuller tone-quality at (b).

Ex. 12: In the *Andante* of the same movement there is yet another type of dotted accompanying figure, upbow, vibrant, rhythmic, resonant, to make a background for the violins:

Andante con moto

Fig. 100

This is continued in the regular four-sixteenths figure, in a *staccato* of a crisp softness, neatly and lightly turned off the bow, again mechanically precise as to up and down strokes (lower portion of bow on account of the double-stops):

Fig. 101

II. The foregoing examples have all been types of detached notes in accompanying figures. *Legato* figures should be subjected to the same sort of inspection and tests in the

search for color, of which they too are a fruitful source.
They too may be treated in several ways. Long, even
strokes of the bow give them a sustained fullness, short,
neat ones a piquancy; the crossing of the bow over the
strings may need to be very distinct so that the notes are
clean-cut, or scarcely perceptible so that they sound almost
like double-stops. The fingering may be purposely chosen
to cross the strings as much as possible, making the groups
distinct, or, when suitable, producing a pedal-like resonance
by an adhesive bow; or it may remain on one string as
much as possible to keep the groups inconspicuous and
smooth.

Ex. 1: In the following instance (Haydn, Op. 76, No. 1)
since the melody is in *piano*, light, a little quaint, and both
it and the accompaniment contrast in dynamic and texture
with the dramatic *forte* unison that has gone before, the
legato eighths should be not too heavy in tone. If done with
short strokes (four notes to a bow, just above the middle
where the bow crosses most clearly) allowing the slight
natural emphasis on the upper, more melodic tones to balance the unison on the low A in both voices, they will give
a live and vibrant, neat, adjustable background:

Fig. 102

(Allegro con spirito)

Here only the viola can use an open string in every other
measure, but where the figure recurs in the second half of
the movement both instruments can make good use of an

open string to keep the characteristic little roll in the accompaniment.

Ex. 2: In the sixteenths figure in the Ravel *Scherzo,* on the other hand, with its triple *ppp* under a *pp* melody, a warbling, blurred background may be effective, very fluent. While clearly pointing the harmonies, bow-strokes and fingering must be inconspicuous (point of bow, near fingerboard, with a sliding motion, very even to conceal crossing of strings where necessary; fingering on one string wherever possible):

(Assez vif-Très rythmé, ♩· =92)

Fig. 103

The above excerpt from Quartet by Ravel used by permission of A. Durand & Cie., Paris, France.

Ex. 3: In the Ravel melody quoted in Fig. 19 a smooth, shadowy background may be laid by the second violin for the strange color of the melody played by first violin and viola. Again, bow near fingerboard, rather windily drawn; fingering by all means on one string, with strong fall of fingers (the harsh tone of the open A would be disturbing).

III.   An accompaniment in a characteristic figure has often to take to itself, where it is prominent, a *soloistic quality.* An introductory measure, or a bridging measure, or perhaps a measure that gives the principal harmonic color, may need to be brought out, still as accompaniment, but with a warmer, more independent and forthcoming tone.

Ex. 1: We are very strict about Beethoven's dynamics, but it may not be out of place, in the *Adagio affettuoso ed appassionato* of Op. 18, No. 1 to yield to the natural tendency of the harmonies by the slightest *crescendo* and *diminuendo* in the introductory measure, almost imperceptible, yet such as to set the spirit of what follows. This would throw the second measure back to its proper accompaniment value, allowing the extremely soft beginning of the first violin's A—like no beginning but a continuation in the actual of something already indicated, inaudibly remote, the first overtone of the opening note in the second violin:

Fig. 104

A similar effect could be made at the altered recurrence of this measure in the second half of the movement.

Ex. 2: In the following bridging measure (Mozart, D Major, K. 499) after the surprise resolution to the relative minor, it is the business of the second violin to define the change in harmony beyond a doubt by the least dwelling on its A—F#—C#. Thus it will lead over to the next phrase with a tone strong enough to cover its solitude yet still consistent with the accompaniment character to which it

must drop back promptly at the entrance of the first violin
with the new melody:

(Allegretto)

Fig. 105

Ex. 3: A fragment of accompaniment in a single voice
may acquire importance because it carries the significant
changes in the harmony. In Fig. 73 (Mozart, K. 421,
Andante) the second violin takes this matter into its own
hands. It may seem that, being the only voice to move at
that point, it already has sufficient prominence, but it is
the *quality* of that prominence which counts; it must be
convincing. The four notes at (a) need the warmth of a
tone soloistic yet proportionate to the other three voices.
Sixteen measures later it is the viola that carries the same
change, and then it should stand out proportionately.

IV. We now come to a more independent type of characteristic accompanying figure, which has an interest of its
own to be considered.

Ex. 1: This interest may be melodic, as in the following
quotation (Schubert, A Minor), with a running fluency that
weaves in and out of the current of the music, giving a

background for the theme yet possessing a color-interest
of its own:

Fig. 106

It is important to bear the color-value in mind throughout,
to change it where indicated by swells and *fp*. The first two
introductory measures perhaps starting not too soft, diminishing, all within the frame of the *pp*, to even less where the
theme enters; soft throughout but not so soft that it lacks
definitely interesting tone quality. It must never sound as
though the player was bored.

Ex. 2: Or the interest may be more distinctly harmonic,
as in the *Larghetto* of the César Franck Quartet, where
the accompaniment is practically a broken chord, giving
richness, solidity of texture—again the organ color. The

massive harmonies pass through a variety of textures. First comes the *ff arpeggio*, supporting the violin's melody, in which every note of the second violin and viola needs to be vibrant and of full value, melodious as well as carrying the chord, yet not overwhelming the first violin's solo:

Fig. 107

Next, the viola is alone, with some support from the cello, as background to the second violin's important line; then again the *ff* passage, diminishing this time to a *pp* in which the second alone carries the characteristic chromatic figure, soft and fluent, fingerboard tone (upper portion of bow) like a whisper, carefully not beginning to increase until two measures later (as the score, not quoted at that point, will indicate):

Fig. 108

The *poco a poco crescendo* now works up gradually through a swimming, even, growing chord to the great sweep of the *ff*:

Fig. 109

After this the accompaniment takes a different form, of triplets against eighths, both melodic figures supporting the harmony, in *piano* (*dolce*):

Fig. 110

Then even eighths again, like an echo in their hollow octaves, *pp* (very soft bow and tight fingers):

Fig. 111

after which the plaintive ascending chromatics of the second violin support the first violin's rising *ppp ma espressivo* line to the return of the original theme in the original key, *sempre ppp*. Here the inner voices can produce an even softer, bell-clear tone in their alternating eighths and triplets:

Fig. 112

The next *forte* passage then leads *poco animato* into the culminating excited *ff* through which, joined by the cello, they deliver swinging triplets, again full in harmony, every note to sound out strong, melodious and vibrant, with firm bow and beating fingers:

Fig. 113

Thus in studying this movement one comes to realize the scope of color possibilities in the quartet texture.

Ex. 3: In Fig. 114 three different types of accompaniment are carried on simultaneously. In the first violin's low theme the second violin works a melodious figure in thirds and sixths (tenths and thirteenths, since they lie in the register above the octave). The dotted thirty-seconds may be played either at the point, in a gentle but clear *staccato* (as marked) or as a long *spiccato* (lower middle, bow taken off between notes), in either case dwelling with a little *tenuto* on the significant melodic tones (Beethoven, Op. 74):

Fig. 114

Meanwhile the viola in its harmonic function must keep a tuneful quality in its gently resonant *pizzicato*, while the cello supplies a quiet off-beat bass with a subdued *spiccato* bow. The whole passage calls for subtlety of ensemble, the second violin, while subsidiary to the first, playing out with freedom—the freedom characteristic of string quartet style, which leaves each instrument its individuality without upsetting the frame of the whole.

Proportion and Relations between Voices

Skill in handling the varieties of color and texture, readiness to think and plan, and critical listening to measure one's achievement as distinct from one's intention are, as we have frequently remarked, most necessary in the quartet player's equipment. He will want to cultivate his sense of the *relative proportions* of the voices to each other under various circumstances, for herein also he will find a fruitful source of color.

I. The proportion one most naturally considers is that of inner voice to leading voice. A downright accompaniment, such as those we have just examined, not only takes on a subordinate quality but molds itself to the voice it accompanies. In modern scores it is often marked with a lesser dynamic degree than the solo, but in older scores, even after Brahms, both or all voices are usually marked the same—*p* or *mf* or whatever—and one or another has to adjust its degree of *p* or *mf*: say, if the accompaniment is altogether subordinate, for background color, it may have to think itself *pp* to another's *p*, or *p* to another's *mf*. If, on the other hand, it is characteristic and possesses melodic as well as background value, it may adhere to the full *p* or *mf*, so long as it does not override the leading voice. In these instances *quality* often accomplishes the end better than actual *volume* of tone.

This is neatly illustrated by a figure in the first movement of Mozart's D Major (K. 499) which is passed quickly frome one voice to another down the range of the quartet. The second violin accompanies the first (a), then switches to solo quality accompanied by the viola (b) which in turn switches to the solo accompanied by the cello (c), the whole series repeated in a two-beat thematic fragment. Second and viola must each finish the one quality before they begin the other as though each were playing on two different instruments; the three solo figures must be handed on in a consistent quality; the three accompaniment figures also. Catching the spirit of this little bit of juggling, one takes pleasure in turning it off skillfully and lightly in the ensemble.*

---

* See also Phrasing, I, Ex. 1, and the role of the second violin in Fig. 10.

(Allegretto)

Fig. 115

(N.B.: The same duet motive occurs near the beginning of the movement but then only twice, handed from the upper to the lower voices.)

II.   While such considerations are fairly obvious in the relation of accompaniment to solo, they also, and particularly, apply to instances of relative strength where *both* voices are of the same, or almost the same, importance. Here again quality often controls the proportion quite as well as volume. One must also bear in mind that a low voice, like the cello or the lower strings of the viola, easily inclines to dominate middle-register tones, and also that the high registers of the violin may be brilliant and penetrating. In short, it is for every voice, in manipulation of color as in the spirit of ensemble, to be ready to adjust itself to what is going on elsewhere in the quartet.

Ex. 1: A case in point occurs after the double bar in the first movement of the Haydn D Major (Op. 76, No. 1). We have heard the theme, now restated by the viola, so often that it is refreshing to hear the counterpoint of the second violin. Like the viola it is marked *f*, but as the register is high it may have to modify its *f* in order not to sound too shrill. Similarly, when the first violin takes up this eighth-note line it should not sound too brilliant against the middle-register tone of the second:

Fig. 116

At the later recurrence of this passage, the sonority of the cello easily holds its own against the first violin, which should, however, be sonorous rather than harshly brilliant.

Ex. 2: In the *stretto* immediately following the measures last mentioned, the second violin and viola, while playing with a vigorous quality that gives character to the argument, should not let their duet in thirds outweigh the single voice of the violin striving upwards with the same figure:

Fig. 117

III. We have seen (Phrasing, II) that it may be necessary in the ensemble to emphasize the voice that has the important statement of the moment, not alone in melody but also in fragmentary figures, bridging tones, or tones that mark a modulation. The value of one tone in a chord may be of the greatest importance to the harmonic and color effect. An augmented or diminished interval, a major or minor third, the tritone, an altered tone, the modulating tone of a progression—in short, the tone that gives a chord its particular interest—must *sound distinctly through the texture* of the four voices in order to give character to the harmonic content, meaning to the musical content, and to carry with conviction to a distance. *Proportionate emphasis* is particularly needed in the case of a *discord* or in that of an *unexpected* progression. The player's own ear will demand that the discordant or unexpected tone be very definite lest it sound like an error, and for the listener at a distance there must be no doubt.

Ex. 1: In the first movement (*Allegro moderato*) of the Ravel Quartet the main theme recurs as at the beginning except for the viola part. The viola (*Tempo I*) repeats its E of the preceding chord, which is distinctly *not* held over the bar but started anew with the phrase itself. It needs to be marked, as with a slight *tenuto*, to convince the listener of the strange color of the E dissonant, otherwise he may assume it was meant to be the consonant F:

Fig. 118

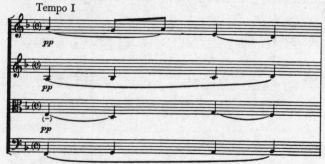

The above excerpt from Quartet by Ravel used by permission of A. Durand & Cie., Paris, France.

Ex. 2: In the long *rallentando* leading to the close of the same movement occurs an example of the import of a single note in the harmony (Fig. 120) where the *ascending* progressions of the first violin are balanced by the *descending* progressions of the viola. As the eighth measure arrives, the color of the chord is lost unless the viola's F♮ (call it the diminished seventh in the dominant of the dominant, prefiguring also the return to the tonic key of the piece) is distinctly heard. In the remainder of the measure also the viola's tones should sound through the rest since they lead to its dissonant B♮ eighth-note (also to be clearly understood) in the F major resolution in the next measure (not shown in our quotation).

String Color

The four strings of the violin, viola or cello have distinct color characteristics which are never so marked as in the clear, homogeneous texture of the string quartet. Here,

as we have seen, each voice moves against a background of
its own kind, while the pure string tone, undisturbed by
admixture of any other type of instrumental tone, is at its
most sensitive. The violin members may acquire the habit
of avoiding the open E if it sounds harsh, but there will be
times when its white brilliance is desirable. * Call the A of
mellow sweetness, the D sombre, the G sonorous and deep.
The viola's A inclines to be nasal, the cello's again is its
lightest string and most amenable to song. The color values
and contrasts of which the sixteen strings of a quartet are
capable are nothing short of amazing, and they demand
much consideration in perfecting the whole color-scheme
of a performance.

Ex. 1: The following eight measures from the *Largo,
cantabile e mesto,* of Haydn's Op. 76, No. 5 present two
distinct phrase-groups in which the most interesting color
and appropriate contrast would perhaps be obtained by
the first violin playing the first group as much as possible
on the light color of the E string and singingly. The second group, however, is an extension of the first measure
without the *crescendo* and lying on the darker D (and G)
strings, and is therefore effective if played without expression, leaving the color-interest to the chromatic descent of
the lower voices in their hollow octave unison, until the
crescendo to *forte*:

Fig. 119

* See further comment on the use of open strings under Intonation.

Ex. 2: In Fig. 54, from the first movement of the same quartet, it is more effective for the first violin to take the four little sixteenths on the D string, after the *fz* on the A, giving them a darker, more caressing tone than would continuation on the A.

Ex. 3: In Fig. 59 the first violin would increase the interest of the color-change from *f* to *p* by taking its first *p* note on the next string: G♮ on the G string after the D string (at recurrence in second half of movement, C♮ on the D string after the A).

Ex. 4: In the coda of the first movement of the Ravel the effective rise in color-value with the rise of the melodic line is achieved by the first violin remaining on the D string through its C♯, so that at the point where the second takes the theme—a point led up to, furthermore, by the crescendo from *pp* to *mp*—its color changes to the lighter tone of the A. Four bars later the crossing to the E string should be made with care because the phrase is *diminishing* and should not be disturbed by any sharpness in the lighter color of the higher string:

Fig. 120

The above excerpt from Quartet by Ravel used by permission of A. Durand & Cie., Paris, France.

Ex. 5: In changing from a flat to a sharp key or from minor to major where the dynamic degree is meant to remain the same, one may need to guard against the slightly stronger tone inherent in the brighter tonality. The (enharmonic) shift from Db minor to A major in the following measures (Haydn, Op. 76, No. 1, last movement) should be made with absolute *quiet* in order to maintain the *pp* and so that the Ab's of the violins are not made to sound like G# resolving into A. In this particular case it is also well to see that the first violin's open A string does not set up a sympathetic resonance to the stopped A♮ , as it tends to do, especially as the change Ab—A♮ is made in octaves with the second violin which already causes a certain additional resonance:

Octaves and the Unison

Octaves and unisons have distinct color-value in string quartet writing. In good writing, that is, where they do not occur out of paucity of ideas or lack of imagination in exploring the four-voice texture but effectively combine the high and low tone qualities or the distinctive individual tone-characteristics of the four instruments. From the player's point of view octaves and unisons are particularly affected by considerations of voice-proportion and string-color such as those just reviewed.

I. Where two voices join to play the same phrase each may need to use less strength than in playing alone, for two promptly produce greater volume than one. It depends, of course, on the context. Then comes another question: Shall the two play equally strongly? Is the higher or the lower voice the more important? Which of the two characteristic instrumental colors shall dominate? For frequently the phrase belongs rather to one than to the other. Let first violins take note: the unison, also the octave, may offer them an opportunity to retire graciously in favor of a colleague.

Ex. 1: The canon form of the *Menuetto* in the D Minor Haydn demands a vigorous *forte* in both voices of each couple, literal, measured, without fine distinctions, only that the lower voices should not be so heavy nor the upper so brilliant as to upset the equilibrium between the two pairs:

Fig. 122

Ex. 2: In the following passage (Mozart, K. 499), while the lower voices will play firmly, rather *more* than *p*, having the melody, the accompanying violins, being in octaves, should play rather *less* than *p*, nearer *pp* in quality. It would seem that the first violin might stand out the more strongly of the two since the register of the second (especially at this second recurrence of the passage) mingles with that of the theme, thickening the lower-voice texture. If the upper octave is supported by its echo, as it were, in the lower, the clear melodic embroidery is pleasantly distinguished against the low melody:

Fig. 123

(Adagio)

Ex. 3: Where the lower violin, on the other hand, has the color best fitted to the rest of the voices, it may well afford to be the more pronounced while the upper recedes to the quality of its higher echo. The second half of Variation VI in the last movement of Beethoven's Op. 74, for example, is cast in a *lower sense* than the first half, emphasized by the cello's insistent D♭, with the duet in sixths and thirds carried on by the inner voices so that the first violin plays the role of higher echo to the second:

Fig. 124

Un poco più vivace. ♩ =76

Ex. 4: The most magnificent example of the cello's domination in an octave passage with the first violin is to be found in the final *Presto* of the last movement of Beethoven's Op. 132 in A Minor, where the cello seems boldly to take away the violin's own high notes (played an octave lower, of course) and forces the violin to give way to its own more passionate power of expression. The passage is too long to quote fully, but every student of quartet playing or composition should acquaint himself with it.

II. Judicious *choice of strings* will assist both voice-proportion and the establishment of color. Two instruments playing in unison in the same register would naturally use the same string. But there are cases where a violin playing with, say, the cello which gives the phrase its characteristic quality, might better *support* the cello's tone on the D string than *imitate* it on the G. Adjacent strings usually combine better than those further apart.

If the second violin in the following example (Mozart, D Major, K. 499) enters in the third position on the D string while the first is playing on the E, an incompatible, almost false tone is produced, while if it simply enters in the first position on the A string there is a smooth mingling of the two violin voices. The viola, in turn, if it enters on the open G string, should guard against sounding too loud in the proportion of the unison:

(Adagio)

Fig. 125

Substance in Tone—The Pianissimo

The relativity and interdependence of volumes of tone have already been discussed, as well as the sort of realistic suggestion which causes us to conceive of a *forte* as full or heroic, strong or merely loud, of a *piano* as significant or small, singing or indifferent. There is one more problem to which quartet players must lend an attentive and critical ear: namely, *the quality of the quartet's tone as a whole.* Merely playing loud or playing soft does not make, at any distance, good tone. The sound may be thin or uneven. Many good organizations fall short of the mark because their tone *lacks body.* That same *vitality* for which the need is obvious in the individual player must be transfused into the quartet's tone. A *real forte* does not happen overnight or by the mere gathering of numbers; it is something to work for,* and when it is achieved the string quartet may rival the organ. The *real piano* that sings *consecutively* among the instruments is not the product of a haphazard softness but a substantial body of sound controllable in a scale of degrees. The *pianissimo* has its own problems: the four voices must be able to make almost no sound and yet that very little quantity must have *quality* or it will be a mere passing of horsehair over sheep's gut.

The reader will have noted allusions to different kinds of *pianissimo.* There is the ordinary *pp* of the straight bow that is merely a *lesser p.* There is the shadowy, vague *pp* produced by the bow crossing the strings very near or over the fingerboard. There is also a cold, white *pp* produced by drawing the bow near the bridge (not so near, of course, as for the feathery *ponticello*). Some discretion is needed in

---

* It is in this sense that Jenö Léner suggests the playing of scales in unison and harmonized, in various note-values and bowing, without and with changes in dynamic degrees. In the short hours available for "playing quartet" most of us want to get right at the music, and unfortunately it does not occur to us to try this sensible practice.

the choice of these. Schubert is apt to mark his melodies *pp*, and he undoubtedly means them to be soft, even very soft. But in both the opening of the A Minor Quartet (Fig. 106) and the announcement of the "Death and the Maiden" theme in the D minor, the *straightforward* soft but melodious *pp* is more appropriate to the style of the music than the more affected color of either the fingerboard or the bridge tone. In music which depends very much on the *merely instrumental* effects of shifting color, however, all possible varieties of *pianissimo* may need to be resorted to. The type of *vibrato* used is also a contributing factor here.

The Vibrato

In the finer aspects of tone quality in the quartet the *vibrato* plays an important role. Too much of it is tiresome, too vigorous oscillation of the four hands does not necessarily make for the best full tone. Also it may falsify an otherwise well-placed tone, for a little more or less of it can affect purity of intonation. A fast, nervous *vibrato* tends to *raise* the pitch. Yet it may serve a good purpose in emphasizing the closeness of an upward chromatic progression where it is hard to place the under finger as high as the pitch demands. Tests of purity are often best made without it: the penetrating clarity of clean intonation may need to be softened by a little *vibrato* but is easily disturbed by too much.

Since it affects tone quality, the *vibrato* is also a factor in production of color. The quartet player will soon perceive that it need not be monotonously consistent, that the slight variations in intensity or speed used so spontaneously in solo playing may with excellent effect be made use of in the four-voice texture—if by agreement, of course, and according to the sense of the passage and the proportionate importance of the voices. The second phrase-group quoted in Fig. 119 (the *Largo* of Haydn's Op. 76, No. 5), for example, suggests a moderation of the *vibrato* to almost nothing in carrying out the hollow, dramatic effect of the descending progressions.

It is also possible to drop the *vibrato* entirely, especially in such *pp* passages as can stand the flat, even tone that results. Sometimes this effect is specifically called for, as in the third movement of Bartók's Fourth Quartet, where the composer indicates at exactly what point the three upper voices, laying down their *pp* background for the cello's solo, are to change their sustained chords from *non vibrato* to *vibrato*. This is a useful device, though not to be overdone; the style of the music will guide one's taste.

Intonation

No combination of instruments more severely tests the accuracy of the players' intonation than the string quartet. The very exquisiteness of texture of its four selected voices is transparent to any defects and just intonation is essential to clean and clear performance.

The string player, making his own tones as he goes along, tempers his own scale. The quartet player, then, has to think of the just intonation of his tones, not in diatonic relation or in relation to each other on his own instrument only, but in terms of the constant, self-engendered process of *modulation* as it is distributed among the four instruments. In other words, their purity is determined by their modulatory relationships. He thinks of an F as *low* when it is the *downward-resolving* seventh in a dominant seventh chord in C or if it forms a *diminished* interval; as *high* when it is the *leading-tone* to G♭ or if it forms an *augmented* interval.

This type of thinking holds throughout, of course. But

there will be passages where particular attention must be paid if the proper bell-like resonance of the "delicious strings"—as Thomas Dekker called those of the lute nearly four centuries ago—is to be achieved. An obvious case would be the opening of the Schubert A Minor (Fig. 106), where the second violin's eighth-notes must establish a clean tonic, soft but of ringing purity against the resonant low fifth of viola and cello. Or the famous "dissonant" opening measures of the Mozart C Major (K. 465), where the bottom seems to drop out of the expected, and unexpected resolutions are brought about through the poignancy of chromatic suspensions and passing-tones. About the intent of those harmonies there must be no doubt: the first violin's A♮ high against the dark C minor background from which the viola's low A♭ still hangs in the ear; then, after the strange move into B♭ minor—G♭, the first's G♮ preparing for the modulation through F to F minor. Or, again, almost any section of Beethoven's Opus 74 (Figs. 78-82). Such purity of intonation is a *sine qua non* in the presentation of contrapuntal music like the preludes and fugues of Roy Harris's String Quartet No. 3 with its many *organum* passages in which the fifths and fourths must come to their effective resonance.

The *quality of tone* produced is important to just intonation. A *forced* tone—a chord loudly struck, a sudden pizzicato, a *fz* or *ff* of barbaric or dramatic effect—will be found to *rise* and may have to be taken lower than if quietly produced. Sometimes the finger is responsible. When placed on the tip, so as to give solid pressure of bone, it makes for a stiffer, harder tone; but when placed on the fleshy cushion it can help to produce a more flexible, softer tone. Sometimes, when about to move to another position, downward for example, the finger relaxes or slips a trifle from its original position and so falsifies the note. Sometimes the answer lies in the choice between the two possible strings on which the notes in question may be played.

Open strings should be watched in this connection, even avoided—unless deliberately good for some special purpose of color—because, in addition to their inexpressive quality, they cannot be tempered and may bring trouble in modulating. Where, on the other hand, the open string sets the tone-effect, as in the F major section (*un poco più animato*) in the third movement of the Brahms C Minor, the character of the passage depends on the ringing open A of the second violin, the other voices centering around this resonance. (See p. 187, Ex. 2 and Fig. 132.)

The *proportionate strength* of the different intervals may also affect the delicate precision of the intonation. A carefully placed chord sometimes retains a lingering impurity of effect which will vanish if a single interval is emphasized a little more, or a little more subdued, in proportion to the whole. It is always well to play *softly* in testing intonation, as impurities are more easily detected in the absence of disturbing variations in tone quality.

In passages where intonation is doubtful or difficult it is helpful to practice two instruments together until they agree, then add a third voice, and finally the fourth. Also, if an individual player has troubles or uncertainties in intonation it will help him to play over the problematic passage slowly against a long note sustained by the cello (or another voice, but the bass gives the best anchorage) until all the tones are clean and clear.*

Tuning

That the four instruments should be accurately tuned to begin with goes without saying. They should take the A

---

* To the late Lillian Littlehales, cellist of the former Olive Mead Quartet, the author will be ever grateful for patient assistance in this respect.

one at a time from the first violin or cello—or from one of the other instruments if it happens to be well played in so that it "has a good A." The two outer voices should agree first. The principal thing is to tune *quietly*, not to draw loud full bows so that the others cannot hear themselves or to seize this moment to walk about delivering snatches of a concerto one is proud to recall. Since not many of us possess perfect pitch, a tuning fork will not come in amiss and this will also help to keep the A on the high side (i.e., not below the standard International concert pitch of 440). The D string is tuned *up* to the A, as the G string then is to the D, and the lower string is best left on the high side of the fifth of which it is, after all, the base. The E string, on the other hand, is tuned *down* to the A.

When apparently clean fifths have been established individually, it is well to check up on the slight inevitable variations by testing open G strings all round and open C's between viola and cello. As in cleaning up intonation, the best results are obtained by tuning *softly*. It is well to form this habit so that any tuning that has to be done before an audience may be as inconspicuous as possible. In public performance, where of course the tuning is done in the greenroom beforehand, it may be necessary to check it on the platform because of change in atmosphere or if someone has a new string, but this can be done by a furtive flick of the fingers or tap of the bow, so that the audience is scarcely aware of it. Any necessary tuning between movements, whether in public or in private, is also best kept as low in volume as possible so as not to overwhelm the ears of fellow players or of listeners with noisy interruption of the music that is under way.

If the ensemble includes the piano or a wind instrument (clarinet, flute, oboe, etc.) the first violin and/or cello should of course take the A from the "guest" instrument.

The Pizzicato

As used in the four-voice texture of the string quartet, the *pizzicato* acquires more importance than in solo music where it appears for virtuosic exhibition or as mere accompaniment, not with any prolonged color significance. If he has had little practice in its use, the new quartet player will have to experiment to find the most satisfactory methods of producing it. He may want to make it dry and snappy or full and ringing. It will sound of the nail unless made with care, and four instruments picking away can produce a most inadequate sound, sometimes an atrocious sound. The finger should *pluck* rather than *pick* the string. Generally speaking, *pizzicato* can be worked into a melodious and sustained effect, with tight finger vibrating the string and quick, accurate action of the plucking finger, and it must always have substance so that it can be molded. It can have many qualities, from dry to tuneful. Like the *pianissimo*, the *pizzicato* is freely used by modern composers in their search for color effects and has accordingly to be treated with all necessary variety. In the *Allegretto pizzicato* movement of his Fourth Quartet, Bartók gives instructions for the effects he wants: from *ppp* to *ff*, or *sul pont.*, or again snatching the string so vigorously that it snaps back onto the fingerboard; chords *arp.* or *non arp.*, or brushed back and forth across the strings, or *glissando* for the cello.

It is largely a matter of individual preference which finger is used, but the first and second fingers and the thumb are capable of characteristic effects. The first inclines most to let the nail be heard, therefore tends to a drier, crisper quality; the second, having more flesh, produces a juicier tone, and it can also be reinforced for strong and quick striking by the thumb placed under its first joint. The thumb sometimes provides a round smoothness in slow consecutive tones, because it can pull off from one string to the next without being lifted, more easily giving a more continuous tone than a finger. There is also a distinction between the action of the plucking finger when the hand is held steady by contact of the thumb with the corner of the fingerboard and when the finger strikes free or with a swing of the hand. On the violin the plucking finger produces a *mellower* tone some three or four inches down the fingerboard toward the left hand (provided the hand is not in a high position, for the length of string between stopping and plucking fingers affects the volume of tone) than near the end of the fingerboard. On the cello a soft quality is obtained, especially in broken chords, by the thumb high on the fingerboard (toward the left hand), whereas for strength on the lower strings in *forte* the best result may be obtained by the finger plucking the string practically where the bow crosses, between end of fingerboard and bridge.

Ex. 1: The *pizzicato* figure from which Beethoven's Op. 74 derives its popular name should be full and resonant, the plucking of the strings on the different instruments so blended and drawn close that the tone, carrying from one to the other, sounds like that of a single instrument (tight finger vibrating the string):

Fig. 126

and so on, through the extension in triplets of quarters, eighths, and triplets of eighths, never losing the full resonance of each tone.

Ex. 2: A sustained tuneful quality (perhaps second finger plucking well down the fingerboard) would be appropriate in the broken-chord accompaniment figure in the *Adagio molto e mesto* of Beethoven's Op. 59, No. 1:

Fig. 127

The cello's eight preceding measures have more varied dynamic significance and would be dealt with accordingly.

Ex. 3: A mellow quality suits the first violin's broken chords in the variation of the *un poco più animato* theme in the *Allegretto* of the Brahms C Minor, perhaps best obtained by the thumb plucking well down the fingerboard until the last *forte* chord, which is not broken but struck:

Fig. 128

Note too, the viola's share in the melody-line with its double A (two fingers, perhaps thumb and middle, and a little *vibrato* on the stopped A so that it rings well with the open A) and the high C of its broken C minor chord.

Ex. 4: A dry quality may sometimes be appropriate, in which the resonance of each tone is briefer, does not carry over so fully as in the preceding examples. This is accomplished in part by the plucking finger but also by less vibration of the finger stopping the string. But care should be taken that this does not degenerate into a mere picking sound. Such quiet dryness seems appropriate in the unusual *pizzicato* variation from the *Lento* of Kodály's First Quartet:°

Fig. 129

It is especially difficult to escape the picking sound where the notes follow rapidly upon each other's heels, as in the *crescendo ed accelerando* measures:

Fig. 130

° Figs. 129, 130 are excerpts from Quartet by Kodaly used by permission of Rózsavölgyi & Cie., Budapest, Hungary.

In fact, where some *quality* is desired in the tone of a quick *pizzicato*, it may be well not to try for too fast a tempo. A very fast *pizzicato* is not only difficult to play but almost of necessity becomes dry and "picky", whereas a slightly less pressing tempo gives a more distinct and more musical effect of liveliness. This will be found to apply to music like the second movements of the Debussy and Ravel quartets, both of which are *vif* and *rhythmé*, lively and characteristically rhythmic.

Chords

In "classical" quartet music, at least, chords of three or four notes—chords, that is, other than double-stops, which have a different function and are treated according to the harmonic significance of their tones—can seldom be handled quite as they are in solo.

With four-note chords, which practically have to be bowed with a break across the strings, two and two, a neatly controlled bow and good ensemble understanding may manage to avoid a scooping effect, which—unless specifically called for (e.g., in Bartók)—is apt to sound sloppy. Even at the close of a movement where large tone is wanted and a sense of finality, the struck-in-one chord often produces more tone than the broken sort one may be tempted to use. Ravel, closing his quartet with a held chord—in which cello and viola have four notes, the violins three—indicates how this is to be executed by writing the lower notes as quarters, to be released, and the upper as half-notes, to be held under the *fermata*, or hold.

In the more usual three-note chord it is almost always important to strike all three notes simultaneously. Their worth is all in the striking and there is no possibility of redeeming their tone after the initial instant; they must sound full-fledged at their inception. Such chords in fact possess more strength than the *arpeggio*, more resonance and carrying power, because of this initial moment in which all the tones sound together.

Absolute precision is necessary in taking these chords: precision of bow on strings, of ensemble, of intonation (lest the vigor of the stroke falsify the tone). They may be given a short, brisk resonance, as in Fig. 57 (opening of Haydn's Op. 76, No. 1) where they are introductory, or a slightly more sweeping resonance as in Fig. 131 (Beethoven, Op. 18, No. 4, first movement) where, though dotted, they are in *fortissimo*, the violins antiphonal. The demands of the music will decide.

(Allegro ma non tanto)

Fig. 131

(Note that a slight backward tendency of the frog—which on the cello amounts to an oblique stroke—evens the notes and counteracts the natural conspicuousness of those on the middle string.)

In *pizzicato* there are, as we have seen, a variety of ways to strike or pluck the strings. The second movement of the Debussy would call for chords struck as much in one as possible. Ravel at a given point in his second movement asks the second violin to play *quasi arpa,* but, again, he writes the final chord as a quarter-note for the cello, two eighths for the viola, and an off-beat eighth for the violins, indicating that the bass chord is to resound through the duration of the others.

Color Value of Tonality

Many prejudices inhere, perhaps, in our conceptions of the color-quality of certain tones, because these are liable to spring from realistic associations which must be individual. But there is a general agreement of opinion upon the emotional effects of major and minor modes, the sombre quality of certain tonalities, the bright quality of others. The certainty of the player's own conception of a tonality— which may be aided by the realistic suggestion alluded to elsewhere—undoubtedly affects his ability to express what he feels (just as it may actually affect his intonation) and thus to inject interest into the color-scheme of the whole, contributing to color value in the quartet.

Ex. 1: In Fig. 105 (Mozart, K. 499, first movement) we have seen the new color emanating from the more sombre tone and more solemn melody which follow upon the merry major.

Ex. 2: A change in color, often caused by a change of key, usually accompanies the contrasting trio in a *scherzo* or minuet movement. After the wistful minor *Allegretto* of Brahms's C Minor Quartet (Fig. 55) comes the major movement, gayer in feeling, where the rolling double A of the second violin emphasizes the mode, the *poco più animato* indicating the livelier spirit, cello and viola keeping up a softly resonant *pizzicato* accompaniment (cf. Fig. 128):

Fig. 132

Ex. 3: Again, in Fig. 39 (Beethoven, Op. 18, No. 1, first movement), at the unexpected resolution to the relative major (Ab) everything contributes to a total change of color-sense: the disposition of the voices, the harping of the viola on the main motive with its low Eb, the suspension-like ninth of the violins at each progression, the marking of the whole, as Beethoven would not fail to mark it, by a distinct dynamic contrast, *pp*.

Combinations with Other Instruments

Although this study has been purposely limited to the string quartet, there is a whole field of chamber music literature in which the quartet player will enjoy applying whatever he may have learned in working in his particular form to the problems of color and texture introduced by combinations of other instruments with the quartet.

The added viola of the viola quintet introduces a highly distinctive color. The added cello of the cello quintet brings other qualities. In the string sextet, where both viola and cello are doubled, the distinction of color is perhaps less acute, but the two violins are thrown into a new relationship with the heavier background, and the treatment of their roles will be modified in certain instances. The octet, or doubled quartet, is again less specific in color but because of its size offers further varied possibilities and the opportunity for larger, miniature-orchestral tone-effects.

Wind instruments introduce other problems of color. The range, warmth, dignity, mellowness of the clarinet endow it with a special adaptability to string tone—different, again, from the cold, clear flute, the heavy horn, the "cranky" oboe which, like the viola, is peculiarly distinctive in tone. Playing with wind instruments, furthermore, provides an excellent opportunity for the string player to grow in his understanding of the art of phrasing. For, as is the case with the singer, the wind player's phrasing is governed by control of that most intimate and organic human mechanism, his own breathing, and it is up to the quartet as a unit to meet his expression with subtlety of ensemble. String players will benefit by the experience of learning—as one did under the tutelage of the late Georges Grisez, an incomparable clarinetist—to "give him room."

Playing with the piano, again, demands other adjustments and degrees of elasticity in ensemble. The percussion instrument brings with it characteristics to which the quartet must be ready to adapt itself, though not those it needs to absorb into its own style. Some ardent quartet devotees like to think that the piano can never enter the sacred precincts of their own art and there is something to be said for the theory. But they would adhere to this prejudice at the cost of missing some of the finest chamber music literature ever composed, and they may comfort themselves in the knowledge that there is much to be learned from experience with the new color and acoustical effects introduced by the percussion instrument which constitutes excellent discipline for the quartet as a unit.

The pianist too has much to learn from the phrasing and sustained tone of the bowed instruments, just as they in turn learn from the singer or wind player. Our piano is a more powerful instrument than Mozart or Beethoven knew, but no matter how modern a work is being played it is chamber music, and the relative balance of his instrument with the quartet is of prime importance to the ensemble. He too must listen to his colleagues, as they to him. He is not a soloist now, as he is accustomed to be, and the noble purpose of the gathered performers will be more easily and sympathetically achieved if he will *consider the strings*: put a book under the lid (if his piano *must* be open), spare the pedal, and observe dynamic marks!

Music Titles in
The Norton Library

Norton / Haydn Society Records

A TREASURY OF EARLY MUSIC

Four 12-inch 33⅓ RPM long-play records to supplement
Parrish's *A Treasury of Early Music.* Monaural and Stereo-
phonic.

Record 1　*Music of the Middle Ages*
　　　　　Examples 1 through 12

Record 2　*Music of the Ars Nova and the Renaissance*
　　　　　Examples 13 through 28

Record 3　*Music of the Renaissance and Baroque*
　　　　　Examples 29 through 41

Record 4　*Music of the Baroque*
　　　　　Examples 42 through 50

MASTERPIECES OF MUSIC BEFORE 1750

Three 12-inch 33⅓ RPM long-play records to supplement
Parrish and Ohl, *Masterpieces of Music Before 1750.*
Monaural.

Record 1　*Gregorian Chant to the 16th Century*
　　　　　Examples 1 through 22

Record 2　*The 16th and 17th Centuries*
　　　　　Examples 23 through 36

Record 3　*The 17th and 18th Centuries*
　　　　　Examples 37 through 50

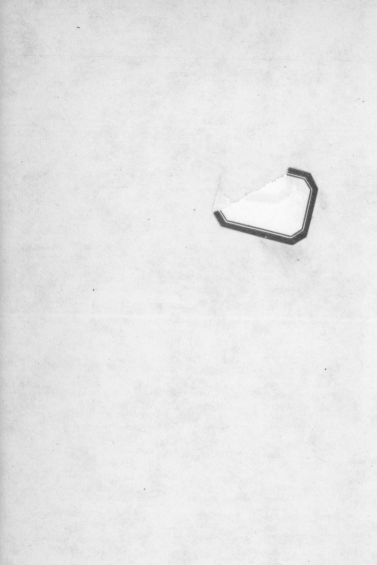